Gardens To Visit
In The West

James Belsey

with drawings
by
SUSANNA KENDALL

REDCLIFFE
Bristol

First published in 1993 by
Redcliffe Press Ltd
49 Park St, Bristol.

Text © James Belsey
Illustrations © Susanna Kendall
Map © Keith Taylor

ISBN 1 872971 87 3

British Cataloguing-in-Publication Data.
A catalogue record for this book is
available from the British Library.

Typeset and printed by
The Longdunn Press Ltd., Bristol.

CONTENTS

The cover photograph of Stourhead Garden is reproduced by permission of The National Trust.

INTRODUCTION

. . . and then, of course, you'll have to write the Gardens To Visit column next summer, I was told.

The column, it appeared, came with my new job as Chief Features Writer of the Bristol *Evening Post* when I was appointed in the late 1970s.

It was autumn then, there were a hundred other things to think about so I quietly forgot about the chore . . . until the following spring arrived.

I knew the column, of course. It was an immensely popular feature in the *Post* and a star vehicle for the late Max Barnes.

Max had established a tradition of writing up a garden which would open to the public the following weekend somewhere in the *Post*'s circulation area of Avon, Somerset, Gloucestershire and Wiltshire. The column ran from Easter to August Bank Holiday, offering readers a thumbnail sketch of the pleasures in store for them if they made the effort to go out and about.

Max was a hard act to follow. What I knew about gardens and plants wouldn't have filled half a page of a small shorthand notebook.

I had two choices, either I could try faking it when I met the garden owners or I could be devastatingly honest and confess a mixture of ignorance and enthusiasm. I did a bit of both that first year.

I still cringe at memories of being asked to admire peonies and walking towards oriental poppies and, worst of all, stepping forward and complimenting one gardener on purple harebells. They were snakeshead fritillaries. All my own fault, but the gardeners didn't mind. They never minded.

Somehow it all began to work. I had a fresh pair of eyes, I saw the gardens and met their creators and heard their stories the way the non-expert garden visiting punters do. And I learnt. Not so much the names of plants – I have almost every journalist's appalling memory for names – but more an increasing appreciation of how skilled, gifted people of taste can blend plants and design and garden features into a place that charms, refreshes, fascinates and adds an extra dimension to our lives.

Within a season I was hooked, never travelling without a

well-worn copy of the famous National Gardens Scheme (NGS) yellow book in the car and often halting on cross-country journeys if I saw the familiar yellow posters announcing a garden to visit that day.

Why this new passion? Because it took no time at all to fall in love with the pleasure of seeing other people's gardens and the sheer fun of the oh-so-English tradition of garden visiting. I love the chatter and the families spilling out over lawns, I like the home-made teas served by volunteers roped in for the day and, best of all, I'm always keen to see how someone else has used plants and made displays which they like and which reflect their character and interest.

This book offers brief sketches of some of my favourite gardens to visit within about an hour's drive of the Bristol/Bath area. They range from the great and the grand public attractions to tiny little private gardens which only open once a year or by appointment.

The emphasis is on the private gardens, because they're the ones I like visiting best. It's always interesting to meet the owners, to hear stories about this plant or that border and to compare notes.

This year's Gardens To Visit column has now gone to bed for the winter but it won't be long before I start thinking of snowdrops and spring as the new season approaches. There will be new gardens to see and old friends to re-visit as yet another garden visiting year comes round.

My thanks to all the gardeners who, in the spirit of true hospitality, want to share their creations with the rest of us and who, in return, win our warm-hearted gratitude and admiration. Long may this tradition linger . . .

James Belsey

GARDENS IN AVON

Algars Manor, Iron Acton

I hate missing Algars Manor in the springtime, but it happens every other year or so and I'm always regretful.

There's something magical about spring in the riverside garden that John Naish has built with its contrasting collection of exotics, magnolias, camellias and rhododendrons.

The site of the manor is older than Domesday – the Saxon lord Algar was dispossessed by the Norman invaders – though the present building dates from 1600. John Naish bought the house in 1950 when working as a consultant at nearby Frenchay Hospital. The house was too big, he admits, but he couldn't resist the garden, part a rather overgrown formal garden with lawns and beds around the house, part a steep sloping bankside along the little River Frome.

He's always loved magnolias and in four decades he has planted and lovingly developed one of the bravest, boldest displays of magnolias to be seen. In springtime the riverside air literally sparkles with clouds of bloom ranging from the pure white of the tall Magnolia Kobus to the starry, red-flushed Leonard Messel.

But that's only part of this riverside extravaganza. Rhododendrons and camellias thrive in the leafy soil and both families of plants have a special place in his heart too, so he has planted them almost as enthusiastically as his beloved magnolias.

The result is magnificent, an opulent flourish of dark, shining leaves and pinks and whites and reds from the camellias alongside the less showy but equally satisfying rhododendrons.

John Naish has carefully created paths down to the river bank and through his plantations so that visitors have the best possible views. There are places to stop and admire the plants and others to enjoy the slinky stream of water and, if you're quiet enough, the many birds that love this little stretch of the Frome.

The upper gardens by the manor are in complete contrast. They have a family, lived-in look about them and in springtime visitors always notice the pale yellow of the Algars Manor oxlips which grow and seed freely from a small collection of seedlings originally collected by John and his wife Barbara from her childhood home in Austria.

The Easter opening at Algars Manor is something of a local institution and hundreds come pouring into the grounds, hoping they'll catch the magnolias in peak condition. If they do . . . perfection.

Algars Manor is in Iron Acton, 9 miles north of central Bristol and 3 miles west of Yate and Chipping Sodbury. Turn off the B4059 Iron Acton bypass, past the village green and down Station Road and over the level crossing. Algars Manor is on the left. The garden is open on Easter Sunday and Monday, April 11th and 12th, and May 16th and 17th. Admission £1.50, children 20p (combined admission with adjoining Algars Mill). Teas. Plants for sale.

Badminton House, Badminton, near Chipping Sodbury

Even the strongest hearts would quail at the prospect of creating a garden in a place as palatial as Badminton House.

The house isn't big . . . it's huge. And, what's more, it is set in the middle of a massive park landscaped in the mid-nineteenth century by Thomas Wright, the so-called Wizard of Badminton.

To make matters even more daunting, Caroline Beaufort had been a cottage gardener by nature and experience when she and her husband made the move from their modest home in the pretty village of Badminton to the great palace up the road when her husband became Duke of Beaufort.

She had learnt to love the colour, informality and typical plants of an unostentatious country garden but it was clear that cottage gardening just wouldn't work in the regal setting of Badminton House.

One thing was in her favour. The previous Duke may have been Britain's leading huntsman but he was no gardener. Caroline Beaufort started with a free hand and almost clear ground.

It wasn't, she decided, a job she felt able she could tackle single-handed so she called in Belgian designer André Goffinet to help mastermind a completely new look for Badminton.

The epic began in the mid-1980s with the marking out and creation of beds and borders, the setting up of new hedges and a massive planting campaign to bring fresh interest and colour.

Today all that hard work has paid off and Badminton now has three splendid garden areas as well as a conservatory and orangery: the open garden just by the house, the more formal area hedged by hornbeam and set a little back from the building with colour co-ordinated borders and its richly profuse rose displays and, finally, the bountiful walled kitchen garden about a quarter of a mile away with its Victorian style archways and other decorative touches.

Roses are the key to the success of these grounds. You'll see them everywhere, not just in that formal display with its very good collection of varieties but also roses which climb, ramble and adorn as many corners of this garden as possible.

And mainly old roses too. She is a great fan of the softer, subtler appeal of the old-fashioned types with their delicate foliage and blooms.

It all adds up to a clever blending of the formal and grand and the informal and personal, giving Caroline Beaufort opportunities to add her own touches with her choice of plants and details but within a solid framework which succeeds well in this historic example of English country house architecture at its most impressive.

Badminton House is 5 miles east of Chipping Sodbury in the village of Badminton. The garden opens for the NGS on June 20th, 2–6 p.m. Admission £1.50, OAPs £1. Teas. Suitable for wheelchairs. Also open to groups by written appointment.

Brackenwood Woodland Garden, Portishead

There are many ways to show off the large exotics like rhododendrons, azaleas, camellias and pieris.

Most of us, with limited space, have to settle for the best we can, which means a corner in a border or even a large container on a patio. And, even more important, planting these soil-fussy beauties usually involves digging a very large hole and filling it with peat or the sort of compost they'll accept.

John and Jenny Maycock prefer the natural look for such forest-dwellers as the rhododendrons and camellias and they allow their plants lots of room to grow in the surroundings of a particularly dramatic piece of English hillside woodland.

The wood is above their nursery and garden centre business in Nore Road, Portishead and it makes for a spectacular sight.

Here, among the silver birch and sycamore, whitebeam and other wild trees you'll find a marvellous range of outsiders including acers from Japan, rhododendrons from the Himalayas, pieris from Taiwan and camellias from China.

John Maycock has been a keen gardener since childhood and acid-lovers like the rhododendrons have always been high on his list of favourite plants. So when he started the nursery and acquired the wooded hillside above which, luckily, has sandstone soil as well as generations of leaf mould, the next step was clear enough – to get cracking on planting out his favourites in a wild habitat.

The Maycocks have opened up a terrace of paths which work perfectly. The wood has magnificent views across the Severn estuary to South Wales and the Welsh hills and these are seen framed by foliage and branches.

Today this most unusual woodland garden has avenues of camellias, mounds of rhododendrons, bursts of red and gold foliage of pieris and the subtlest shades in a handsome collection of acers. The trick works perfectly. This isn't a Himalayan hillside but it almost could be in some corners where you find rhododendrons looking completely at home and at ease, almost as if they were born to grow and prosper in this corner of Portishead.

There are decorative features too . . . a Japanese-style bridge over water, a thriving bog garden, wide, grassy

pathways, numerous pools and waterfowl and a very good collection of rare and unusual shrubs and trees.

A little bit of the East on a wooded hillside in the far west. . .

Brackenwood woodland garden is in Nore Road, Portishead on the Clevedon coast road. The woodland garden is open from mid-April to September, 11 a.m. to 4.30 p.m. Admission £1, children 40p. Plants for sale.

Church Farm, Lower Failand, near Bristol

When the Slades began making their garden on a small-holding at Church Farm in the hamlet of Lower Failand, almost no one had heard the phrase organic gardening.

That was back in 1974 when the pile-on-the-chemicals brigade still ruled the roost. How tastes change! Yesterday's eccentrics are today's leaders and a generation of gardeners like the Slades have taught us to return to traditional methods and to respect nature.

Norman Slade remembers from his boyhood when the Failand area was dotted with thriving little traditional market gardens which supplied beautiful vegetables and free-range poultry for the well-off folk of Clifton, a short journey away.

So when the couple moved to Church Farm he had a heritage to recall . . . and a clear desire to create a really exciting garden which would use the best plants and be made with tried and true methods.

Garden-visiting enthusiasts in the Bristol region make an annual bee-line to Church Farm because it's forever changing. Norman and Jean Slade are never content to stand still . . . and their enthusiasm shows in this busy 2¾ acre grounds.

The soil is almost neutral so both ericaceous and non-ericaceous plants can be grown. There's a large organic vegetable garden on the raised bed system and there is a recently established rose garden featuring all their favourite roses.

A water garden is a must and the Slades have their own complete with pools and specimen Koi carp which swim majestically through their domain.

Almost two decades of growth have given this garden mature shrubs and rapidly maturing, interesting trees including metasesequoia and ginkgo. Visitors love the so-called 'secret garden' with its acers, magnolias and other good trees.

The Slades are specialists too, with representative collections of several plants including clematis and rarer varieties of the popular osteospermums.

Above all, Church Farm is one of those cheerful, attractive, busy private gardens which is a joy to visit, whether you're a keen-eyed specialist or someone who loves admiring someone else's labours. Either way, there's enough to make this an excellent garden to visit.

Church Farm is 6 miles south-west of Bristol. From Bristol take the B3128 Clevedon road. At the crossroads in Failand opposite the garage turn right down Oxhouse Lane to Lower Failand and park by the church. The garden is well signed on open days. From the M5 take exit 19 (Gordano) towards Bristol and immediately turn right into Portbury. Leave the village on Portbury Lane and turn left into Failand Lane. Church Farm opens on Saturday and Sunday May 22nd and 23rd. Plant stall, cream teas. Admission £1, children 25p. Wheelchairs possible. Also open Sunday June 27th, plant stall but no teas.

Crowe Hall, Widcombe, Bath

I know several veteran garden visitors with impeccable taste who consider the hauntingly atmospheric grounds of Crowe Hall one of the best, most romantic gardens of all.

Not for wonderful plants or perfectionist beds and borders, not for great displays of flowers and shrubs but instead for Crowe Hall's unforgettably beautiful position and its magical blend of architecture, formality and natural wildness.

One look is enough to tell you that this was a garden created in the days of large gardening staffs. It is a big, hillside garden stretching in all directions from a large, airy, classically styled house built in 1927 after a disastrous fire destroyed most of the earlier house except for the mid-Victorian portico and great hall. This is a garden which would take at least half a dozen pairs of hands to keep neat and tidy. Well, there aren't, so the more formal areas receive the most attention while nature has taken over in other places.

It isn't difficult to imagine what Crowe Hall's garden must have been like in the old days: spotless beds, neat displays, sharply defined borders and immaculately groomed shrubs. I think I prefer it today.

14

The formal lawn and pond garden, reached past balusters and stone steps in front of the house, is a charming period piece which leads to a little stone bridge and the much wilder terrain beyond.

Follow a paved path through woodland and past a Victorian Gothic grotto and you're in the open again and enjoying a charming little Italianate garden with breathtaking views, notably to Prior Park.

Below are zigzag paths down the steep hillside through a sequence of little terraced gardens and to another side is a roomy area with beds filled with favourites like cranesbill geraniums, phlox and peonies.

Above the house is pretty parkland with good trees and spring displays which add yet another touch of magic to this eyrie-like place.

This place is gardened with love and affection and a great deal of effort, but not with the numbers of staff to bring off the sort of effects for which it was designed.

That matters not a jot. This sleeping beauty has more to offer than a dozen manicured, neat grounds.

Crowe Hall is one mile south-east of Bath. Turn left up Widcombe Hill just before the White Hart on the A36 and the garden is up the hill on the right hand side. Crowe Hall opens Sundays April 18th, May 9th and 23rd, June 6th, August 15th. Admission £1, children 30p. Teas.

Goldney Hall, Clifton, Bristol

The great gales of January 1990 ripped swathes through Bristol as trees fell by the thousand. The news from Bristol's most historic garden, the eighteenth century pleasure grounds that the rich merchant Thomas Goldney had built on the Clifton hillside, wasn't good. Three huge beeches felled, the yew avenue shredded . . . it sounded like a catastrophe.

But it wasn't. That hour of mayhem ripped open the veil and let light pour into this fabulous garden the way it hadn't done for more than a century. The balance had been altered suddenly, dramatically and for the good.

It's no wonder that leading garden lovers like Prince Charles make a bee-line to Goldney Hall, now a Bristol University students' home, whenever they are in Bristol. It is a gem.

Thomas Goldney was a Quaker merchant who made a fortune from two incredibly successful voyages of the Bristol privateers the Duke and the Duchess, enough to build the house and garden of his dreams up in Clifton, well away from the muck and grime of the city centre.

The garden was developed between 1731 and 1768 by his son Thomas Goldney the younger who ordered himself some fabulous follies . . . a subterranean cave sparkling with semi-precious stones and shells brought back by his captains from distant beaches, a romantic tower, a peaceful canal . . . and he had terraces and lawns and avenues created so he and his friends could promenade and enjoy the view across the smoky city and busy docks below, to the hills and rolling landscape beyond.

Bristol University's gardening staff have been lovingly restoring the grounds, removing modern plants and replacing them with ones Goldney would have known. Year by year the eighteenth century details are being recovered and restored. Goldney's beauties are brought into sharper focus every year.

A charming parterre with low box hedges has been developed by the canal, there is a meadow of wild flowers deliberately kept uncut until later in the summer and one of my favourite spots is the walled garden where a wide range of shrubs and flowers familiar to eighteenth century gardeners are grown.

Each season sees a busy programme of private parties
using the wisteria-clad Orangery as the centrepiece and
Thomas Goldney would have thoroughly approved of
Bristol University's policy of letting out the garden for
functions. This is, above all, a pleasure garden, perfectly
suited for wedding receptions, anniversaries and the like
where guests can stroll and wander or just sit in corners and
admire one of England's most classically beautiful places.

*Goldney Hall is on Lower Clifton Hill, at the top of
Constitution Hill, Clifton, Bristol. The garden opens April 25th
and May 2nd, 2–6 p.m. Admission £1.50, OAPs and children
75p. Teas. Also open to groups by written appointment.*

Harptree Court, East Harptree

Discovering buried treasure in your own garden must be the greatest childhood dream of all . . . and for Richard Hill the dream came true.

Richard Hill of the famous Hill shipowning, shipbuilding company had childhood memories of underground tunnels at the family home at Harptree Court in the Chew Valley.

But it was only when one of England's leading architectural historians, Tim Mowl, called in to take a long look at Harptree Court that he realised the family had been sitting on a fortune in their lovely country house garden.

Not in abandoned family jewels. Not in hoards of Roman coins. Not even in a buried cache of priceless china. No, instead there was something much rarer hidden beneath the surface. Nothing less than a secret tunnel and grotto system created by fanciful garden architects in a more romantic age.

Tunnels, grottos and follies of every sort were the ultimate status symbol when Harptree Court, set among woodland with lovely views over the Chew Valley, was being built in the late eighteenth century by Harcourt Masters, then the City Architect of Bath.

And its owner, 'L. Scrope Esq', decided that he wanted the very best the landscape and garden architects could offer with a beautiful bridge, stone-lined streams and underground world.

Richard Hill began by discovering the pleasure of restoring the stonework of the pretty stream through his grounds. Then his thoughts turned to memories of dim and dark caverns and a tunnel nearby. He recalled being warned to keep well away from the rather spooky underground workings . . . which made them all the more attractive to a small boy. He did explore one or two shadowy corners but both ends of the tunnel had collapsed and the middle filled in with rubbish.

Dr Mowl examined old plans of the house and garden when he came to Harptree Court as part of a listings exercise of interesting buildings in the Bristol area. He saw a mention of a 'subterranean passage' which reminded Richard Hill of childhood days and those gloomy corners.

They went to examine the place. Those rubble-filled earthworks proved to be the folly garden's finest feature, but by now impassable thanks to years of dumping rock, earth and even old milk churns in an effort to keep children away from the dangers of a roof fall in such a confined space.

The tunnel is open once more to excite the curious visitor, the stream sparkles, the bridge is set in the middle of a handsome, mature garden with lovely trees and Harptree Court has all the charm of the fine eighteenth century pleasure garden it was originally designed to be.

And to add a touch of their own, the Hills have had their own late twentieth century – but very eighteenth century in mood – Doric temple built to continue the tradition.

Harptree Court is 8 miles north of Wells in the village of East Harptree on the Mendip side of Chew Valley lake. Harptree Court opens June 13th, 2–6 p.m. Admission £1, children free. Teas. Plants for sale. The garden is suitable for wheelchairs.

Hillside, Coombe Dingle, Bristol

Hillside is one of those large, romantic, old-fashioned town gardens that garden lovers dream about. It is two acres of peace and beauty in the Bristol mini-suburb of Coombe Dingle.

The area is named after the steep little woodland valley just below Hillside and the house's title reflects its position halfway between the glades below and Kings Weston Down above.

This garden's original layout is Georgian and the bones of the grounds, the walls, paths and main tree planting date from a couple of centuries ago. The mood is elegant, charming and leisured and if you turned a corner and bumped into a group of characters from a Jane Austen novel, they'd seem perfectly in place in this delightful two acres of shade and sunshine, lawns and flowers.

The garden was re-worked in Victorian times, giving it at least one very interesting feature, an ornamental rose garden dug in the rough shape of the letters C and T for the woman who lived there, Catherine Tebbs.

Today another Catherine gardens at Hillside, Mrs Catherine Luke, a devoted, experienced and sensitive gardener who has

19

the happy knack of blending a sharp eye for detail and order with just the right amount of tolerance for informal and even wild areas in these grounds.

Hillside is a superbly mature garden. Its architecture, particularly the walled kitchen garden, is beautifully weathered and the trees planted all those years ago now create a magnificent setting.

She loves good shrubs and collects unusual flowering plants but she is just as happy to allow honest-to-goodness rampagers like Honesty and forget-me-not to seed freely. This is a big garden, after all, and there's room for a little laxity.

Special allowance has been made for peat-loving plants by burying old baths and wash boilers up to their necks and filling them with peat and the well planted rockery adds extra interest.

Hillside is particularly beautiful in springtime when the good trees and shrubs are just coming into leaf and the spring flower displays are at their best, showing off this fine garden to perfection.

Hillside is in Grove Road, Coombe Dingle. It opens May 3rd and 4th, 2–6 p.m. Combined admission to Hillside and the nearby Pennywell with its magnificent flowering cherry and views across the Blaise Castle estate is £1. Children free. Teas. The garden is suitable for wheelchairs.

The Manor House, Walton-in-Gordano

Simon and Philippa Wills are plantsmen. They collect plants, just as a philatelist collects stamps or an art lover paintings and sculptures – but they're plantsmen with style and an excellent eye for creating attractive effects with leaf and flower.

The Wills present their plants as beautifully as they can in their large, four acre garden between Clevedon and Portishead, just as the art lover will show a painting in the best place and light. They seek out rarities on foreign travels, from other collectors and from rare plant catalogues and they learn all they can about the botanical lineage of their collection. They catalogue each plant and use a computer to annotate the information. Hardly surprising with several thousand different plants.

Plantsmen are special. They have a discipline that's much more demanding than most collectors face because their collections are alive and need a great deal of care and attention. Their passion for their plants shows in a series of brilliantly presented displays which offer lots of object lessons for visitors on the look-out for new plants for their own gardens.

The Wills began serious gardening in the sloping four acre grounds of the attractive manor house at the Clevedon end of the pretty Gordano valley in the mid-1970s. There wasn't much of interest apart from a handful of mature trees including a Monkey Puzzle tree planted in Victorian times which is now so tall that it makes you dizzy to stand beneath and look upwards.

The collection and garden grew as they cleared, re-designed, used the woodlands of the upper part of the grounds for more shade-loving favourites and created great pools of colour and interest among the open lawns below. Ponds form the centrepiece of a rectangular terrace between lawns and are the nearest thing you'll find to formality in this light, welcoming garden. The rest is pleasantly arranged around lawns and paths in a sequence of fascinating displays showing plants big and small at their best.

One glance is enough to tell you that this is a plantsman's garden. It's those labels lurking on or by each well-loved plant, labels which remind and inform and save visitors the trouble of asking what is this or that. The Wills do it with subtlety but efficiency.

Springtime sees wonderful bulbs, the summer marvellous herbaceous displays and the autumn a succession of late flowering gems before the reds and yellows of leaves and berries as winter approaches. There's even interest in the deepest midwinter. This is a garden in its prime.

The Manor House is the first house on the Clevedon side of Walton-in-Gordano between Clevedon and Portishead on the B3124. The garden is open from mid-April to mid-September and mid-October to early November, Wednesdays and Thursdays from 10 a.m. to 4 p.m. and on Sundays/weekends April 12th, May 2nd and 3rd, June 6th, July 25th, August 29th and 30th. Admission £1, accompanied children under 14 free. Coaches by appointment throughout the year, telephone Clevedon 872067. Plants for sale. The garden is suitable for wheelchairs.

Parsonage Farm, Publow, near Pensford

Parsonage Farm is a woodland garden for all seasons and a garden which offers highlights at any time of year.

The early spring sees the flowering of one of the most interesting and varied collections of snowdrops you will find in the area and they make a beautiful sight set against the leafless trees. As a contrast, there is a very wide range of hellebores, from the palest to the almost black flowered types.

Next come spring bulbs in great profusion before the shrubs, decorative trees and flower beds and borders come into their own with particularly good aquilegias of every colour to give highlights in many corners.

The setting is particularly attractive. The three-and-a-half acre garden is on a hillside overlooking the little River Chew. It is very well wooded with some unusual trees, rarities introduced by a previous owner who travelled the world in the tobacco industry and made a habit of collecting seeds and planting them on his return.

Today Parsonage Farm is the home of Andrew Reid and his plantsman wife Norma. When they came to live here they brought with them a collection of about 100 favourite plants.

That original collection included rhododendrons and azaleas which thrive well in the leaf mould rich soil of this woodland garden and have matured over the years, adding good dashes of colour in the dappled light alongside a grand collection of the best shrubs.

Clever paths provide a whole succession of large and small vistas, from shadowed glimpses seen through leaves and branches to a stunning view across fields to Publow church.

Nothing goes to waste in this garden. Seeds of favourite plants are lovingly collected and raised, self-sown seedlings are treasured, cuttings are carefully grown on and many of the younger trees you will find in this garden were raised from seeds.

Even garden waste and dead timber finds its uses, building up fresh beds and providing the framework for new terracing.

Nearer the house the woodland gives way to a more open garden which includes a heather garden and rockery as well as nicely-planned displays of all the summer favourites, particularly roses.

Parsonage Farm is in Publow, 9 miles south of Bristol. On the A37 Bristol-Wells road turn left at the top of Pensford Hill, almost opposite the B3130 to Chew Magna. The entrance is down the lane about 250 yards on the right. Parsonage Farm is open by appointment, telephone 0761–490229 and a charge of £1 will be made, to be donated to the NGS.

Pear Tree House, Sherborne Green, Litton

It is no wonder that the popular TV gardening show 'Gardener's World' chose to run a special feature on the garden which John and Pamela Southwell have built over the last quarter of a century at their home at Pear Tree House.

Sherborne Garden, as it has become known, is as perfect example of the enthusiast's garden as you will find anywhere. Years of thought, care, design, skill, plantsmanship and sheer hard slog have gone into transforming a scruffy patch of neglected land into a magical world of plants and colour.

The Southwells began with three-quarters of an acre to work with, but the garden has grown and grown along with their increasingly wide range of knowledge and enthusiasms for new branches of gardening. Today Sherborne Garden is almost four acres, a grand creation divided into a series of cleverly landscaped compartments to reflect different moods and atmospheres.

The water garden is a feature most modern gardeners fear, worried at tales of all the problems that can beset ponds and streams. The Southwells' large ponds and moisture gardens show brilliantly what can be achieved with ambition and hard graft, offering visitors a chance to see a lovely display of water and damp-loving plants set against the attractive reflections of the water itself.

The flowers are grand and there are flowers for all seasons . . . glorious spring displays, the best of the summer blooms with species roses given pride of place and, in autumn, an extra special effort to prove that the season of mists and mellow fruitfulness can have petals too, colchicums (autumn crocus), cyclamen and many other September/October gems. And as for fruitfulness, take a look in autumn at their collection of hollies . . . more than 180 varieties and almost certainly the largest collection in the south west.

You will find a strong emphasis on good and often unusual trees. A pinetum is now flourishing and there are collections of birches and acers, the latter particularly valuable for those reds and yellows to add the finishing touches to the autumn show.

This is an endlessly fascinating garden, one to be visited again and again as the seasons go by to see how the Southwells have managed to find yet another range of plants

24

to make their cleverly-worked garden one packed with interest throughout the year.

And, luckily, that is what you can do because Sherborne Garden opens frequently, attracting many regulars who love the sight of such a well-designed, expert plantsman's country garden.

Sherborne Garden is 15 miles south of Bristol, 7 miles north of Wells on the B3114 Litton-Harptree road, half a mile past Ye Olde Kings Arms. Sherborne Garden opens Sundays and Mondays June 13th to September 6th, also April 11th and October 10th, 11 a.m. to 6.30 p.m. Admission £1.50, children free. Plants for sale. Teas. The garden is suitable for wheelchairs.

Portland Lodge, Lower Almondsbury, near Bristol

So this is what a professional garden designer's own private garden looks like.

That's the remark that is made time and time again when Nada Jennett and her architect husband Fred open their compact garden to the public.

She is an outstandingly talented garden designer and lecturer. He is one of the region's senior architects and his buildings include the dramatic Roman Catholic Cathedral church of St Peter and Paul in Pembroke Road, Clifton.

The views from their garden are stupendous, with the great sweep of the Severn below, the Forest of Dean and Welsh hills beyond and, on clear days, the mountains of the Brecon Beacons.

That is the plus side of their home and garden. On the minus side are the winds that come whipping off the Atlantic and up the Bristol Channel . . . straight into their garden. And if plant-damaging winds weren't enough to contend with, Portland Lodge has very heavy wet alkaline soil thanks to some ten feet of clay beneath.

When the Jennetts began gardening here in the 1980s, they found a pretty bleak terrain. The winds knocked plants

PARK GARDEN CENTRE

The "Out of Town" Garden Centre

Over Lane, Almondsbury, Bristol BS12 4BP

Telephone Almondsbury 0454 612247

The Gardener's Garden Centre
for all seasons
and for all your gardening needs.
Expert advice

We are a
Hillier
Premier Plant
Agent

OPENING TIMES:
Monday to Sunday
Seven Days a Week
Winter 9am - 5pm
Summer 9am - 6pm

down, it was too cold to sit out of doors and plants rotted in winter in the clay soil.

So first came shelter with a fast-growing hedge, then the importing of loads of shingle to bring drainage to the clay and then, at last, they could tackle the more pleasant job of planting.

The garden is designed to create a sheltered haven in this very open landscape, so it has been divided into three distinct levels with circular lawns surrounded by densely planted mixed borders of small trees, shrubs and perennials.

She likes big plants, roses, the more compact trees and, one of her trademarks, the taller Euphorbias which were given to her by the late Margery Fish, that outstanding gardener/writer whose garden at East Lambrook Manor is described in the Somerset section.

She enjoys plants which ramble and climb and spread around her paths and lawns and the result of all this intense planting is an often spectacular series of displays within a limited space. It's very romantic, very clever and full of ideas for us all to imitate.

Turn off the A38 Bristol–Gloucester road to Lower Almondsbury at Over Lane, about half a mile from the M4/M5 Almondsbury interchange. Turn right at the war memorial, down the hill and then left into Pound Lane and left again into Knole Close. Portland Lodge opens Wednesday April 28th, 2–6 p.m. Admission £1.

9 Sion Hill, Clifton, Bristol

Town people with restricted back gardens and a distinct lack of courage – and I'm one of them – should see what Craig and Kay Begg have made of the walled area behind their home in Sion Hill, Clifton.

The front of this elegant Georgian house has one of the most stunning views of any town house in Europe, over the Avon Gorge and directly across to Brunel's Clifton Suspension Bridge, barely a couple of hundred yards away.

But behind the tall, terraced house is a garden typical of so many in this period part of Bristol. It is small with tall walls. When they moved to the house in the mid-1970s there were

27

three trees, a rotting gas cooker and that was pretty well that as far as the garden was concerned.

The Beggs weren't novices. They'd picked up plenty of useful advice and information from expert friends as they built their previous garden, again a town garden in Bristol. They learnt to love roses, particularly old roses.

They had growing children so they grassed over much of the area in the first years. But as the children grew older and play space became less and less important, they began planting in an increasingly busy programme of plant collecting.

After a while the garden had plenty of fine plants but too little shape – so in went a hefty, rugged pergola, paved areas, rose arches, brick paths and even a central herb garden with formal, patterned beds. It was at this stage that the Beggs' garden really began to be very special.

The pergola offers shade and height and a clear division between the terrace by the back of their home and the garden beyond. Favourite climbers have raced up the woodwork, roses, honeysuckles and, above all, a vigorous Clematis Armandii. This leathery-leaved beauty loves everything about its Clifton home and it has grown and grown and grown into a spectacular example.

The paths give nice touches of formality just as the rose arches are pretty staging posts on walks around the garden. And all around are beds and borders packed with good plants which thrive in the sheltered atmosphere created by the tall walls and the garden's sunny aspect. The collection of old roses look perfect in the height of summer.

Nearer the house are plenty of large containers packed with colourful and interesting plants – and within easy reach of the watering can during those dry spells!

This lovingly, lavishly planted secret town garden is so well designed that it's full of surprises as you step from one part to the next, offering all-the-year-round interest and pleasure.

And it's an object lesson to us all. Be bold, plant freely, build paths and raise pergolas. Then you'll achieve the effects the Beggs have made so dramatically.

9 Sion Hill opens on June 6th, 2–6 p.m. in conjunction with other Clifton gardens. Combined admission £1.50 adults, 25p children. Plants for sale. The garden is suitable for wheelchairs.

Bracken Hill, University of Bristol Botanic Garden, Leigh Woods, near Bristol

If Bristol University Botanic Gardens sounds a trifle formal and academic and you have a mental picture of a sort of outdoors botanic lecture theatre, then visit Bracken Hill in Leigh Woods to discover one of Bristol's most interesting grounds.

This extensive garden and showy Victorian house perched above the densely wooded slopes of Leigh Woods on the western side of the Avon Gorge once belonged to W. Melville Wills, a member of the great Bristol tobacco family. The Wills were a family of keen, dynamic gardeners – they thought nothing of having huge horse-drawn wagon loads of Mendip peat brought to Bristol so that they could grow plantations of acid-loving rhododendrons.

This grand three acre garden was built into a series of formal and informal areas and it boasted some of the finest hothouse orchids in the West Country, lovingly grown by the large gardening staff in Mr Wills' glasshouses.

That's all a memory now. The house was taken over by the Air Ministry during the Second World War and instead of floral displays being planned in its elegant rooms, experts set to work on designing wartime airfields.

The Agriculture Ministry followed and by the time they'd finished running crop experiments in the grounds, there was precious little left of Mr Wills' masterpiece.

Today Bracken Hill is very much a garden again. Bristol University took over the place after the agriculture scientists had departed and, over the years, botanists have brought together one of the finest collections of species plants you'll find.

The garden has been organised to allow the widest possible range of plants so there are damp and wet areas, a meadow for wild spring and summer beauties like local orchids, formal corners and a generous amount of greenhouse space.

Look into the greenhouses and you'll discover exotics like insect-eaters, giant cacti and sensitive leaves which curl at the slightest touch. Tour the grounds and you'll find poisonous plants in special corners – beware the poison ivy – showy shrubs and trees and a beautiful range of flowers from every corner of the world and from every part of the plant kingdom.

The garden also manages to have a healthy local accent thanks to a policy of tending local rarities like the Bristol sorbus, the Cheddar pink, the Bristol onion and the white rock rose from Brean Down.

Labelling is excellent throughout the garden so you're never at a loss as you come across yet another unusual beauty – and there are more than 4,000 species to show visitors the extraordinary diversity of the Earth's flora.

Bracken Hill is in North Road, first right after crossing the Clifton Suspension Bridge. The garden is open Monday to Friday from 9 a.m. to 5 p.m. NGS open days are July 11th and September 12th, 2–5 p.m. Plants for sale on charity days. The garden is suitable for wheelchairs. The garden is supported by the 'Friends Scheme'. Members enjoy a quota of surplus plants and seeds and access to the garden at weekends. Annual membership £10. Telephone 0272–733682.

The Urn Cottage, Charfield

The cottage garden that Lesley and Alan Rosser have created at their home in Charfield, a mile or two below the Cotswold edge, is a triumph of small garden design.

Everything in this limited space is just so, from the neat, decorative and very productive kitchen garden to the beautifully worked flower displays which are such a feature of this attractive three-quarters of an acre.

The position is excellent. The house and garden stand between a banked stream and open fields with lovely views to the Cotswolds hills beyond. The three-quarters of an acre appears to fall naturally into a series of attractive areas.

Naturally? Not quite so. It's almost impossible to believe that when professional garden designers Lesley and Alan Rosser moved to their Charfield home in 1982, there was almost no garden at all. They didn't start this garden with fork and spade – they called in the heavy brigade to clear the worst features, to whit one JCB which gouged out half a dozen hefty elm tree stumps.

And then came the planting and the building as they made paths, borders, compartments and a host of features.

The paths are all made from real paving stones and slabs lovingly collected over the years. A raised bed by the house has been cleverly constructed out of abandoned railway sleepers and you'll find many examples of that sort of inventiveness throughout this remarkable garden. The house is surrounded by containers bursting with flowers.

In high summer the couple's magnificent collection of roses are the scene-stealers, clambering up through trees and along pergolas, scenting the garden deliciously.

Flowers and plants are grouped with care, with loose colour themes offering a great deal of variety as you step from one part of the garden to the next along paths and around corners, and plants have been chosen to give all-year interest in a sequence of densely planted displays.

The stream bed has been used as an attractive feature, adding the sparkle of water to give an extra dimension to one side of the garden. Whether you're looking for ideas on how to make a herb bed pretty or thinking of a water garden, planning a pergola or considering paved paths, this garden offers all sorts of good ideas.

The Urn Cottage is 19 Station Road, Charfield, three miles west of Wotton-under-Edge. In Charfield turn off main road at the Railway Tavern then 400 yards on left. The Urn Cottage opens on May 30th, 12–6 p.m. Admission £1. Teas. Plants for sale. The garden is also open to groups by appointment throughout the year, telephone 0453–843156.

Vine House, Henbury, Bristol

The garden Tom and Anne Hewer built on scrubby land at Vine House in the Bristol suburb of Henbury has enchanted and educated visitors for decades.

There are now two or three generations of good, keen gardeners in the Bristol area who learnt invaluable lessons from the Hewers' experience, good taste, botanical knowledge and hospitality to garden visitors. This is the Hewers' inheritance and it will last well into the next century.

Vine House is a good garden at any time of year but spring is my favourite moment, when the great Magnolia Kobus which dominates the main lawn bursts into bloom against a hard blue sky and when the dappled, uncut grass below the mature shrubs and trees becomes a sea of blue Scilla Cernua with dashes of white and yellow. Blue and white are favourite Hewer colours in springtime. Yellow they use sparingly, limiting themselves to sparkles from tiny wild daffodils and the subtler shades of wild primroses.

Then come the famous Hewer peonies near the house, in muted shades of yellow and pale reds and now so free-seeding that seedlings cluster along the edge of pathways to be lovingly dug up and taken off triumphantly to new gardens. I've (quite inaccurately but no less fondly) labelled mine Peony Hewer to remind me of the pleasures of this lovely garden.

The story started with a massive bonfire on VJ night in 1945 when the Hewers, both very knowledgeable gardeners, burnt all the scrub and brambles at their new home before calling in students armed with sticks and string. The two acres run level before a sharp dip to a stream by the Blaise Castle estate. The sticks and string were moved from place to place as the Hewers mapped out their grand planting plan and a little artificial stream introduced to make moist places for water lovers.

Half a century later the Magnolia Kobus, one of their first plantings, is a giant and other trees, often unusual and frequently raised from nuts collected in special places on visits abroad, are mature. Some original shrubs have been replaced as time catches up with Vine House.

The Hewers have collected many plants from the wild in places as far apart as France and Afghanistan and the emphasis throughout the garden is on species rather than hybridised plants just as the mood of this cleverly landscaped garden is completely informal.

The attention to detail has blurred a little over the years but the atmosphere of this hauntingly beautiful town garden is unforgettable. I was drinking cider on the lawn one summer evening when there was a growl through the trees and a huge hot air balloon floated into view almost above our heads. So peaceful, so secret is this garden that the balloon had crept up unnoticed until the final seconds.

Vine House is in Henbury, 4 miles north of Bristol city centre on Henbury Road, next to the Salutation Inn. The garden opens April 11th and 12th and May 30th and 31st. Admission £1, children 30p. Plants for sale. The garden is suitable for wheelchairs. Also open by appointment, telephone Bristol 503573.

GARDENS IN
GLOUCESTERSHIRE

Alderley Grange, Alderley, near Wotton-under-Edge

Long-distance Cotswold Way walkers who pause in the village of Alderley on a warm summer's day when there's moisture about may find themselves enchanted by the scents of this picture postcard place.

And I'll bet those fragrances will have come wafting across to them from Guy Acloque's lovingly tended, lavish garden at Alderley Grange. This garden becomes more famous by the year and it deserves every last bit of praise lavished on it.

The garden has a marvellous pedigree. It was originally created in the 1950s when Alvilde Lees-Milne, garden writer and designer to the great and famous – clients included Mick Jagger – lived here. She had help and advice from an even more famous expert . . . no less a person than Vita Sackville-West, that genius of twentieth century gardening. It was Mrs Lees-Milne who planted the magnificent main border.

Guy Acloque and his family moved to Alderley Grange from London in 1974, already something of an expert on plants thanks to his keen interest in herbs, which he defines as plants with culinary or medicinal properties. He has stamped his own personality and talents on the grounds.

His love of herbs offers him a vast array of useful plants, from tiny, creeping thymes which give off powerful scents when crushed by passing feet to shoulder high lovage and from the colourful range of salvias like the very attractive Salvia Tricolor to the lesser-known varieties of such kitchen favourites as mint, parsley, oregano and onion.

Herbs suggest flavours and scents and that theme of growing scented plants is one of Alderley Grange's great attractions. Guy Acloque doesn't actually ban scent-less plants from his large, sunny, walled gardens but his heart lies with those which offer more than just leaf and flower.

As well as his beloved herbs he also collects old-fashioned roses from all the best nurseries as well as the most interesting fragrant climbing plants and scented shrubs, continuing the Alderley Grange theme of fragrances. Parties of blind garden lovers are especially welcome here and are encouraged to crush leaves and hold flowers during their visits.

The framework of the garden is excellent with good hedges, Cotswold stone walls, well-made paths and leafy avenues. His philosophy is to keep paths clear and pristine but to plant closely and generously. Plants are allowed to climb and flop, spread and ramble and it's only when they start becoming a nuisance that they are curtailed.

This happy, friendly, busy garden has one extra bonus. It's a thrilling place to be in showery weather, the rain bringing out even more fragrances than on sunny days.

Alderley is two miles south of Wotton-under-Edge. From Wotton follow the signs to Alderley, from the A46 Bath–Stroud road turn north-west at Dunkirk and through Hawkesbury Upton to Alderley. Alderley Grange opens on Sunday June 20th. Admission £1.50, children free. Plants for sale. Parties by written appointment during June. The garden is suitable for wheelchairs.

Barnsley House, Barnsley, near Cirencester

Barnsley House is ten minutes or so beyond this book's geographic boundaries – of gardens within an hour's drive of Bristol – but those few extra minutes are well worth the effort.

If you arrive in the early summer when Barnsley's laburnum walk with its architectural underplanting of allium is in bloom, you'll almost certainly recognise the sight.

That avenue, those round allium heads, the creamy yellows of the laburnum and the deep, shadowed greens below . . . you've seen it all before? Well, almost certainly. This must be one of the most photographed corners of any English country garden. It has appeared in scores of books and magazines across the world.

Barnsley is now a mature garden, the creation of the gifted garden designer and writer Rosemary Verey whose clients include such noble neighbours as Prince Charles at nearby Highgrove.

It is a brilliant showpiece at any time of year, a labour-intensive display which no amateur gardener could possibly hope to match unless they became a slave to their plants, shrubs and trees. The beds and borders almost always look perfect, but that's because plants are moved in and out in a succession of planting to ensure the greatest possible interest throughout the year.

What I love about Barnsley is Rosemary Verey's talent for decoration. She led the way in reviving the idea of making a kitchen garden attractive as well as workmanlike by her use of formal beds and flowers alongside veggies planted in attractive groupings.

Another of her pioneering moves was to build an intricate little knot garden, reviving a centuries-old English tradition and, in the process, starting a new fashion. There are now dozens of knot gardens growing up and down the country thanks to her inspiration.

Rosemary Verey has a very good eye for colour and colour combinations in this roomy four acres and she has developed a series of atmospheric areas, from the cool of the laburnum walk with its pebbled pathway to the sunny open prospect by the eighteenth century summer house.

I was once at Barnsley when a party of American enthusiasts on a grand tour of the best English gardens happened to call by. I suppose it must have been because I'd been seen chatting to one of the gardeners that one American, mistaking me for one of the staff, came rushing up to shower me with thanks for Barnsley's beauty. There wasn't time to explain as she rushed away. Barnsley has that sort of effect on visitors . . .

Barnsley House is in the village of Barnsley, 4 miles north-east of Cirencester on the A433/B4425. The garden is open on Mondays, Wednesdays, Thursdays and Saturdays, 10 a.m.– 6 p.m. throughout the year. Admission £2, OAPs £1, children free. Plants for sale. The garden is suitable for wheelchairs.

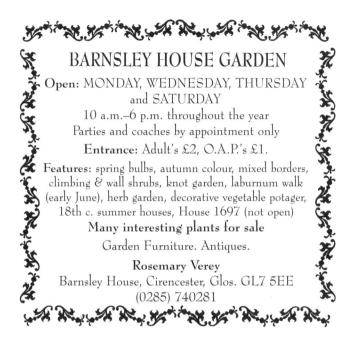

Beverston Castle, Beverston, near Tetbury

Beverston Castle is one of England's most extraordinary architectural gardens . . . how many can boast a genuine, twelfth century ruined castle inside the garden wall?

But that's exactly what Beverston boasts and it's amusing to think of the eighteenth and early nineteenth century romantics who built mock ruins and phoney temples when you come here. This is the real thing!

The ruin towers above the grounds like a gothic theatre set while one corner of the garden dives deep into the bed of the great moat which once surrounded the fortifications. To add to the sense of unreality, there's even a very nice-looking eighteenth century Cotswold stone house built into the remains. It's the home of keen gardeners Major Lawrence Rook and his wife Jane.

The setting, they say, is everything and that's almost true. Almost but not quite. In the 30 or so years the Rooks have lived and gardened in this fabulous showpiece, they have added some delightful touches of their own.

Wisely, they've used wide lawns and open light to take maximum advantage of the almost melodramatic appeal of the castle. But they have also skilfully added interest and colour to the scene.

The scrubby little areas of grass which once surrounded the house have been replaced by interesting paving, giving the right sort of architectural feel to complement such good buildings. The paving is Cotswold stone to match the surrounding architecture and cracks between the flags are planted with low-growing thymes which add interest and scent if they're crushed by passing feet.

One more recent patio off at a corner of the house gives a little bit of privacy in what is a fairly public garden – it's just by the main Tetbury–Dursley road and the ruin is such a landmark that most passers-by can't fail to notice and stare at the sight. This secluded area is surrounded by good walls covered with nice old roses.

There are well-planted borders both around the lawns and the house itself. The lawn borders feature the best of the good old favourites like Tradescantia, day lilies and hosta.

And around the house there is plenty of planting, with long-flowering hydrangeas, tall, stately euophorbias and splashes of white from osteospermum.

When visitors get over the sensational setting, they notice two repeating colour themes, gold and white. The gold comes from plants and shrubs chosen for their bright foliage while the white is worked through a series of flowers, particularly in early summer.

Beverston Castle is 2 miles west of Tetbury on the A4135. The garden is open by written appointment all year and for special NGS openings. Plants for sale and teas at some openings. The garden is suitable for wheelchairs.

Brackenbury, Coombe, Wotton-under-Edge

Peter and Margaret Heaton are truly gifted gardeners who combine a love of abundant, colourful displays with a deep interest in botany and the garden they have built at Coombe in a hidden valley by Wotton-under-Edge is a delight.

It is a plantsman's garden but one built with a rich sense of design and an atmosphere of richly bountiful informality.

When they bought the house with its half acre grounds at the end of the 1970s, they began by studying the soil. They found loam in most of the garden but also a hefty deposit of clay – kindly dumped by the builders when excavating for the foundations of the house.

This gave them plenty of opportunity for variety in their planting and they have since created a series of small, densely planted mini-gardens up and down the half acre, from a tiny bog to a very cleverly designed orchard and from the pool to tidy veggie beds on the deep-bed system.

The orchard is a good example of the care they take. It works like this: because the lowest part of the garden is prone to the valley frost, they have planted the trees in order of tenderness. At the top you'll find the pear trees, then plums and then apples, not only practical but also very attractive when the trees are in full leaf.

But the real strength of this country garden is the magnificent range of happy, healthy shrubs and perennials – the Heatons have no qualms about moving a shrub time and time again until it looks and feels at home.

This process of trial-and-error has brought a marvellous sense of natural design to Brackenbury with flowers and foliage blending just so. But the garden doesn't stand still – it is always evolving and there are always new projects in hand.

Because the garden has so many compartments and because the plants have been arranged so cleverly, it has many object lessons for gardeners with gardens big and small.

The Heatons can boast more than 300 different types of hardy perennials living happily side by side with more than 130 different sorts of shrub . . . and all in apple pie order.

They love growing plants from seed and cuttings and do it very well, raising even the most difficult plants with apparent ease. But don't fret or feel jealous, they always offer a good range of their plants for sale for charity on their open days.

Brackenbury is 1 mile north-east of Wotton. From Wotton Church take the Stroud road B4058 and half a mile along turn right, signed Coombe. The house is 300 yards on the right. Brackenbury opens on June 27th, July 25th and August 30th. Admission £1, children free. Plants for sale. Teas.

The Chipping Croft, Tetbury

Greater love had no couple for their box hedge than that they transported it more than 100 miles when they moved home!

And that's precisely what Peter and Juliet Taylor did when they decided they'd had enough of London and globe-trotting and chose to settle into the peace of a leafy corner of the lovely old Cotswold town of Tetbury.

They had lived and worked overseas but had a good garden at their home base in Hampstead . . . and that good box hedge. So good, in fact, that when they began moving

42

west they brought it with them. They still fondly recall their first night in their new home. All they'd brought was a mattress to sleep on and 35 carefully packed box plants.

The story illustrates the sort of care and work the Taylors are prepared to put into gardening and they have certainly worked hard since arriving in Tetbury.

The shape of this garden is most unusual. The attractive seventeenth century Cotswold stone house nestles at the bottom of Chipping Hill, below Tetbury's market place, and it stands just by what was once a quarry but is now the garden area, two acres of walled town garden on three levels.

Dominating the scene is what was once the quarry floor and is now a beautiful, lush green lawn surrounded by tall, mature trees which give the place a very dramatic setting.

Above that are a series of painstakingly, lovingly worked terraces in a succession of formal areas, from the burgeoning, very well designed fruit and vegetable garden to such attractive formal features as the water garden with its water lilies and goldfish.

Recently added features include an attractive potager of vegetables and flowers, a luxurious potting shed/summer house and courtyard in the 'middle' garden and a sunken patio. This garden never stands still!

Everywhere you look you will find good and often unusual plants among the generously planted shrub and herbaceous borders. There are roses a-plenty and, in springtime, there is a strong emphasis on spring blossom and the best of the spring bulbs.

Chipping Croft is on the left hand side at the bottom of Chipping Hill which leads down from the market place with its car park. The Chipping Croft opens on April 25th and June 6th and 13th. Admission £1.50, children free. There are plants for sale and teas. The garden is also open by appointment, telephone 0666–503178.

Hodges Barn, Shipton Moyne, near Tetbury

Never be confused by the name of Hodges Barn, near Tetbury, one of Gloucestershire's best gardens to visit. It isn't a barn and it certainly doesn't stand in a farmyard.

No, the mis-named barn proves to be a deliciously flamboyant piece of late fifteenth century architecture and the surrounding acres have been transformed into a garden which skilfully blends traditional English styles with some very original touches.

This most unusual place, now the home of keen gardeners Charles and Amanda Hornby, was built in 1499 as a huge columbarium or dovecot where the local squire raised and fattened pigeons for the table.

The nesting boxes are inside the domes of the Barn and the doves used to provide meat for countless pigeon pies and other goodies to be eaten at the nearby great house.

Well, the great house went up in flames in the mid-sixteenth century but the grandiose dovecot survived, stranded and unattached in rural Gloucestershire.

It has had a very chequered history since then. It fell into disuse as a working pigeon roost and has been a cattle shelter and a toolshed.

But then, half a century ago, it was bought and converted into a very unusual country house. The Second World War held things up but in 1946 the outline of the present garden was designed, built and planted.

Some Italian ex-prisoners of war, awaiting repatriation, lent a hand with the architectural features and if there's a noticeable Italianate airiness in their Cotswold stone walls and terraces, that's the reason.

Today's garden has 1940s bones, but Charles and Amanda Hornby – he is the grandson of the original owner of the rebuilt house – have stamped their own personalities on these eight acres since they began a serious restoration in the early 1980s.

The garden had an enclosed, private, inward looking atmosphere before 1980, offering a series of rooms within a room. The Hornbys have turned that inside out. Their home is surrounded by beautiful, open Cotswold countryside so they have cleared and opened and created vistas to the world outside.

There are many features to admire, like the very unusual tapestry hedge, good, well-planted garden borders, attractive beech hedges, sparkling lawns – Charles Hornby claims he has the best lawns in Gloucestershire and I won't argue – a woody, wild flower garden, a large pond with water garden and deliciously cool groves.

The garden is lovely throughout the year but especially so during the magnificent spring displays and in June and July when the roses are in full bloom. These are the times when the Hornbys' clever planting around their strikingly unusual home is seen at its very best.

Hodges Barn is ¼ mile on the Malmesbury side of the village of Shipton Moyne, three miles south of Tetbury and a mile or so south of the Hare and Hounds crossroads on the Bristol/Bath to Tetbury main road. Hodges Barn opens each Monday, Tuesday and Friday 2–5 p.m. from April 1st to August 1st. Admission £1.50, children free. Also open by written appointment. Plants for sale. The garden is suitable for wheelchairs.

Hunts Court, North Nibley, near Dursley

When I first went to Hunts Court, in the shadow of that lovely wooded Cotswold edge hill topped by the Tyndale Monument, Keith Marshall reckoned his collection of old-fashioned roses numbered perhaps a couple of hundred.

It's two or three times that number now and if you want to see old roses given head room, climbing room and the sort of space they love, you couldn't do better than to visit this extraordinary garden.

Keith and his wife Margaret were dairy farmers working from a farmhouse where, it's reputed, William Tyndale was born. The man who first translated the Bible into English and was martyred for his pains is commemorated by the tall tower which looms far above the garden and makes such a striking feature on any journey along the nearby M5.

Keith's interest in roses began in a small way and then, like the plants themselves, grew and grew. So much so that farming began to take second place to those roses . . . and he kept moving his garden fence into the adjoining fields to make more room for more plants.

Happily, the Marshalls' passion coincided with a quickening public interest in old-fashioned and species plants – particularly roses – which started in the 1970s and had already become more than a passing fad by the mid-1980s.

Today Hunts Court boasts 500 and more species, old roses and a thriving nursery business too. The roses are piled in huge, generous displays which are way, way beyond what most of us could cope with in our own gardens, but that makes Hunts Court even more attractive.

There are rampant climbers and ramblers which streak 40 or more foot up trees or along trellises and the clever planting, with an eye for foliage and colour, ensures interest in a superb display which reaches its climax in the height of midsummer in June.

Catch the right moment when there's dampness and warmth from a fresh burst of sunshine, and the scent of this garden is almost overpowering. Roses aren't the only plants, of course. The Marshalls collect all the best old-fashioned garden plants and they've raised a fine collection of very good shrubs and trees as the bones of their garden.

The floral displays are well-presented with a series of lawns to open the garden and to allow the dramatic views up to the Monument and across to the beautiful Stinchcombe Hill above Dursley.

There's plenty for any garden-lover to enjoy on a visit to Hunts Court but for rose lovers in general and specialist rosarians in particular, Hunts Court is a must.

Hunts Court is just outside the village of North Nibley. From Wotton-under-Edge take the B4060 to Dursley, turning right by the Black Horse inn in Nibley and then bearing left at the fork after 400 yards. Hunts Court and the nursery are open all year, Tuesday to Saturday except August, garden 2–6 p.m., nursery 9 a.m. to 5 p.m., plus NGS openings on the last three Sundays in June and first two in July. Admission £1, children free. Also by appointment, telephone 0453-547440. The garden is suitable for wheelchairs.

Lydney Park Gardens

Just across the Severn bridge and then along the west bank of the Severn a few miles, taking in those lovely west-to-east views of the Cotswold edge, you'll find a very special garden at Lydney Park. It is large, wooded and, at certain times of the year, one of the most colourful woodlands in England.

It was created thanks to a spur-of-the-moment piece of inspiration by the then owner, the late Viscount Bledisloe, in the early 1950s.

Around the house is a formal garden which looks across to Stinchcombe Hill above Dursley. Beyond that there is a wooded valley . . . and it was in this valley that Lord B, as he was affectionately known by his staff, noticed that a small clump of rhododendrons, planted years before to hide an unsightly waterworks, were doing rather well.

Land on which rhododendrons thrive in this region dominated by limestone is rare indeed and he decided to make the most of a soil which has become acid through centuries of leaf-fall. He brought two gardeners down from London to plan, clear and plant the eight acres of woodland with exotics.

More than three decades later this epic piece of planting by Lord B and his two associates has produced a garden that is brilliant in colour with display after display of rhododendrons and azaleas cleverly planted to complement mature trees, a stream and two lakes.

The exotic shrubs follow colour themes, blues, pinks, yellows, reds and whites in handsome succession and all on a carpet of green undergrowth and, in season, spring flowers. The bluebells are always magnificent and April and May are probably the best months to visit Lydney.

Walks have been created and surfaced, leading visitors to more and more viewpoints in and around the valley, showing the garden to its best advantage.

Lord B and the team planted for the future, reckoning that their work would reach its full glory at the turn of the century. But it was already lovely in his lifetime.

During the great drought of the 1970s Lord B spent hours toiling up and down the valley priming pumps and keeping the woodland watered and his labour of love limited the losses, but sadly he suffered a heart attack after one particularly strenuous session.

He died three years later in 1979. He was showing a close friend around the garden he had created and helped to save when he suffered his final heart attack.

There is an attractive memorial to him in the little folly that overlooks the best of the displays. It was his favourite spot.

Lydney Park also boasts a Roman camp and temple site, excavated by Sir Mortimer Wheeler. The adjoining Roman museum's greatest prize is the Lydney Dog, a Romano-British bronze considered one of the finest pieces of sculpture of its period.

Lydney Park is on the Chepstow–Gloucester A48 road between Aylburton and Lydney. The garden is open each Sunday and Wednesday from Easter to June 6th and daily between May 24th and 31st, 11 a.m. to 6 p.m. Also by appointment for parties, telephone 0594-842844. Plants for sale and teas. House not open.

Brackenwood Woodland Garden

Barnsley House

Misarden Park

Stancombe Park

Westonbirt Arboretum

Hodges Barn

Clapton Court

*Tintinhull House. Reproduced by kind permission of The National
Trust Photographic Library/Mike Warren*

East Lambrook Manor

Lackham Gardens

Sheldon Manor

Pound Hill House

The Minchinhampton Gardens, Minchinhampton, near Stroud

The Minchinhampton trio of St Francis, Derhams House and Lammas Park have been one of the region's most popular garden visiting venues for years and it isn't difficult to see why.

When two or three keen sets of gardeners get together in an attractive village and they offer teas and picnic places as well as their gardens to visit, the afternoon turns into a get-together for everyone, those who enjoy a day out as well as the keen garden lovers on the look-out for ideas.

The Minchinhampton trio have become so popular that for several years their charity opening has been the biggest one-day money raiser for the National Gardens Scheme in Gloucestershire, a magnificent achievement in a county so rich in private gardens.

The setting here is dream-like, three adjoining gardens overlooking a beautiful Cotswold valley and encompassing eight acres of prettily designed beds, borders, lawns and displays in a lively, colourful mix of ideas, themes and interests.

Mature trees give St Francis, a modern Cotswold stone house, a grand backdrop, particularly the fine beech avenue leading to the house itself.

The terraced garden is packed with good things to admire, not least Mrs Mary Falconer's striking collection of bonsai trees, many lovingly grown from seed, which surround the house.

All plant lovers will approve and admire Peter and Mary Falconer's well-worked borders. He is an architect and it shows in this garden's good overall design. Both are plantsmen in a quiet way, bringing together a very wide variety of plants to create a rich tapestry of foliage and colour.

The borders are also a grand feature of the Falconers' neighbours Mr and Mrs Byng at Derhams House and Mr and Mrs Grover of Lammas Park, with the former also boasting a good water garden and very attractive spring displays of crocus and snowdrops.

Lammas Park's jewel is its wild garden and restored 'hanging garden' on the sharply terraced edge, taking every advantage of the spectacular views of its dramatic position.

From Minchinhampton's Market Square go down High Street then right at the crossroads and, 300 yards along, bear left. The gardens are down the hill on the left. The Minchinhampton trio open on March 14th, April 4th, August 1st and 2nd. Admission £1.50 for all three gardens, children are free. Plants for sale. Teas. St Francis is also open by appointment, telephone 0453-882188.

Misarden Park, Miserden, near Stroud

The Cotswolds has a goodly sprinkling of beautiful manors and handsome manor gardens but there is something extra special about Misarden Park, near Stroud.

This is a garden in which architecture and design come together perfectly in terraces, topiary, lawns and dry stone walls. It is a place of true English garden elegance with the added interest of charming formal and informal displays of flowers.

The garden stands high, overlooking the lovely Golden Valley and it must have been the position which attracted the builders of the original seventeenth century manor house. The house was enlarged and added to by that outstanding early twentieth century architect Sir Edwin Lutyens, a man who believed that houses and gardens should be part of the same overall design.

The grounds, as you will find on a visit to almost all 'Ned' Lutyens' creations, are there to set off the house as elegantly as possible, and here the plan works perfectly.

This is a garden to enjoy and today these large grounds have become a thriving public attraction, opening regularly during the week in the spring and summer season and, occasionally, at weekends.

Visitors find a pleasing mixture of the formal and the informal. Around the house are noble lawns, sculptured topiary, a magnificent yew avenue, herbaceous borders packed with good flowers and a very well restored rose garden.

Further away are the wilder features which come into their own in springtime when aconites, snowdrops and early lilies flower among the uncut grass.

Adjoining the garden is a good nursery where visitors can buy plants as keepsakes of what is always a delightful garden to visit.

If you're puzzled by the two spellings at the top of the page, Misarden with an 'a' Park and Miserden with an 'e' village, so are we all. The spelling difference is a local curiosity which has stuck over the years.

Misarden Park is 7 miles north-east of Stroud and is off the B3070 Stroud–Birdlip road. The garden opens each Wednesday and Thursday, April to September, 9.30 a.m. to 4.30 p.m. and on April 4th and July 4th, 2–6 p.m. Admission £1.50, children free. The garden is suitable for wheelchairs.

Newark Park, Ozleworth, near Wotton-under-Edge

I once visited Newark Park in the mist. The day was dull, the sky overcast. The Cotswolds looked damp and chilly above Wotton-under-Edge. Then, as I drove up the steep road leading past Wotton, fingers of mist formed and joined into an opaque cloud. Headlights on, I crawled my way to the Elizabethan hunting lodge which has been Robert Parsons' home for more than two decades.

We had had coffee and were walking through the hall lit by a large window when a shadowy figure suddenly loomed out of the murk outdoors and there was a heart-stopping shriek like someone being murdered. It was a peacock, perched on a column. Robert Parsons rather enjoyed my discomfiture.

But then the mist fell away, the haunted atmosphere vanished with it and suddenly I was seeing one of the greatest garden views of this region. No wonder the Poyntz family chose this dramatic Cotswold cliff top when they built their hunting lodge here in the sixteenth century . . . and no wonder that its Texan tenant has a love/hate relationship with the house and garden he has been restoring for the National Trust.

Some gardens thrill for their sheer location and Newark Park has one of the best. Its dramatic position offers a sensational panorama across south west England and the ten acre grounds of terraced woodland has been designed to take full advantage of them.

The house, which was made into a four-square castellated country house by James Wyatt in 1790, has a small, semi-formal garden around it but the real attraction is springtime in the woodland with its lavish displays of cyclamen, spring bulbs and carpets of aconites among the grass.

There's a fanciful castellated folly in the woodland, a lake and some pretty paths but you're advised to wear wellies if the weather has been at all damp. This can be a very moist place.

If the weather is clear when Robert Parsons holds his spring open days, bring a pair of binoculars too and have the fun of spying out details of a view that has inspired visitors for four centuries.

Newark Park is 1½ miles east of Wotton-under-Edge and 1½ miles south of the junction of the A4135/B4058. The garden opens on April 4th, 2–5 p.m., admission £1, children 50p, and from June to September, Wednesday and Thursday afternoons by prior appointment only, telephone 0453-842644, admission £1.50, children 75p.

Painswick Rococo Garden, Painswick

In 1757 Bishop Pococke visited Painswick House and wrote, 'Mr Hyett has made a very pretty garden . . . it is on a hanging ground in the vale and on a rising ground on the other side.

'All are cut into walks and through wood and adorn'd with water and buildings'.

And, in case that description does not offer the sort of detail you might like, there is even a painting of Mr Hyett's remarkable garden, painted nine years before the Bishop came to see the place for himself.

It shows a perfect Rococo garden of avenues and follies, water and geometric designs and all neatly woven into a little Gloucestershire valley looking across to the Cotswold edge.

The name Rococo comes from 'rocoille' which means rock work and it refers to bizarrely shaped rocks and other natural objects with which eighteenth century pleasure-lovers used to embellish their gardens. As far as gardens are concerned, 'Rococo' has come to be applied to eighteenth century whimsical, asymmetric pleasure grounds designed to delight the eye of the visitor.

This particular Rococo garden vanished as the centuries went by, disappearing beneath woodland and brambles, old man's beard and leaf mould. The folly buildings fell into disrepair and nature took over.

Until Lord and Lady Dickinson, scenting a new mood of interest in historic gardens, decided to restore what they were assured was England's only surviving perfect Rococo garden. That was in 1983. Today the garden is a magnet for keen visitors from across the world.

Bulldozers went to work first, tackling the back-breaking task of clearing the wilderness, bringing back light and preparing smooth surfaces for the next stage, planting. Grass went down, hedges were planted and vistas were opened up as part of an epic operation.

Thankfully there were grants available from English Heritage and expert advice from the Georgian Society and the Garden History Society as the buildings were restored and garden re-planted as accurately as possible. Water features were re-introduced. Now, almost a decade later, the garden is a gem, a beautiful place to walk and reflect and enjoy a place of great aesthetic order.

It is lovely all year but late winter and very late spring are very special, the former for the dazzling snowdrop displays and the latter for those magical weeks when fresh leaves and clear light add the perfect sparkle to the place.

Painswick Rococo is well signposted and is half a mile north of Painswick, near Stroud, on the B4073. The garden is open Wednesday to Sunday, February 1st to mid-December and Bank Holidays, 11 a.m. to 5 p.m. Plants for sale and teas.

Stancombe Park, near Dursley

Lovely Stancombe Park is one of those places the keen garden visitor should not – repeat not – miss.

Here are two of England's most enjoyable private gardens rolled into one and gardener Mrs Gerda Barlow's open days are a by-word for those who love the atmosphere and the beauty of Stancombe Park.

This isn't just a gentle garden visit. It's a real adventure for the whole family.

There are two quite separate gardens at Stancombe, one modern, the other historic with the two linked by a narrow, raised flagstone pathway which winds its way down a spectacularly beautiful Cotswold valley to a narrow, tunnel-like entrance which seems to lead into pitch darkness.

But take a deep breath, plunge into the darkness and within a step or two the daylight is more brilliant than ever and you've entered the secret world of Stancombe's fabulous pleasure garden with its romantic lake, paved avenues and fascinating follies like the arch made from the huge rib-bones of a whale and a neo-classical Temple.

Why that tiny, forbidding entrance to this hidden wonderland? Well, the story goes that it was deliberately designed in the old days by Stancombe's slim owner to keep his overweight wife at a distance while he dallied with his beautiful gipsy girl lover inside the secret world.

It's as good a story as any in a story-book garden and, fittingly, the scene helped inspire one of the best-known novels of the twentieth century, Evelyn Waugh's *Brideshead Revisited*. Not only did Waugh write great chunks of Brideshead sitting outside the Temple, he also devoted some of his lushest prose to describing the folly garden in front of him, using them as his model for his fictional stately home. Brideshead fans who know Stancombe can soon find the key passages.

The upper garden is a delight, a clever piece of modern design which uses fairly elaborate plantings to dazzle visitors with its elegance. But you'll find homely effects too. The wide, rockery-like border by the house should convert even the most doubtful to the exquisite beauty of foxgloves, white and purple, blended with rarer beauties.

Other features, like the avenue which takes advantage of the stunning view up to Stinchcombe Hill above, the generous tree and shrub plantations and the neat beds planted intricately with baroque swirls of little box hedges around blue/purple plants add to the strong sense of decoration at Stancombe.

Stancombe Park is half-way between Dursley and Wotton-under-Edge, just off the B4060. The garden is open on June 13th, 2–6 p.m. and by written appointment for parties. Admission is £2, children 75p. Teas, plants for sale. The upper garden is suitable for wheelchairs.

Westonbirt Arboretum, Westonbirt, near Tetbury

Westonbirt Arboretum isn't strictly a garden but there isn't a tree or foliage or autumn colour lover in the Bristol/Bath area who hasn't made the pilgrimage to this very special place at least once.

Autumn brings the biggest crowds and for the showiest of reasons. The autumn colour is fabulous, blazing reds and oranges, shimmering yellows, the subtlest shades of pale green and near-brown . . . all of them coming together in a famous display that draws visitors from across the country in that last moment before winter sets in.

The arboretum was begun in 1829 by Robert Stayner Holford who lived in the big Westonbirt House nearby. He started planting trees for pleasure and the tradition continued until 1951, by which time a grand collection of now mature trees had been established.

Five years of neglect followed until the Forestry Commission agreed to take over this wonderful woodland in 1956. Restoration was followed by a busy programme of planting and planning to make the arboretum a visitors' attraction. Today its amenities include an excellent visitors' centre complete with exhibitions.

These days more than 170,000 people visit the arboretum annually and most of them make the trip in the six weeks from the end of September to mid-November.

A walk through the fiery foliage of The Link in Silk Wood demonstrates exactly what it is that brings the crowds. Two superb collections of maple trees were planted here in the 1970s and 1980s to add to the arboretum's existing National Japanese Maple Cultivar collection in Acer Glade.

The Link's leaf display features more than 200 maples, planted in groups and now well into maturity. Catch them on the right day and it looks as if this corner of the woodland is on fire.

The range of colours is magnificent. The delicate seven-fingered leaves of these truly beautiful trees range from the deepest copper and green throughout a succession of fiery reds to dazzling yellows and oranges.

But don't be utterly seduced by Westonbirt in the autumn time. Those who enjoy softer tones should visit the

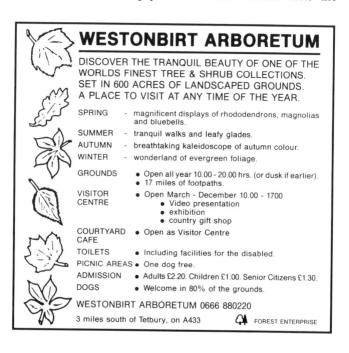

arboretum in springtime when the trees are just starting to come into leaf. In its quieter way, that is just as magical as the famous autumn shows.

Westonbirt Arboretum is on the A433 Bath to Tetbury road. Westonbirt Arboretum is open from 10 a.m. to dusk. Admission £2.20, OAPs £1.30 and children £1.00.

Westonbirt School, Westonbirt, near Tetbury

Step into the grounds of Westonbirt School and you walk straight into a Victorian fantasy of wealth, power and opulence.

This extraordinary garden, now listed as a Grade One garden of national importance by National Heritage, was the creation of Robert Holford.

He was so wealthy, so powerful and so determined to create a showplace to impress visitors that he even had the nerve to move the entire village of Westonbirt a mile or so from the mansion he was building because he felt the sight of all those villagers and their humble homes would spoil his view. Only the parish church was allowed to remain, as a sort of architectural folly for his garden.

Holford spent a breath-taking £200,000 on his country house in 1868. Work that out in today's money and you'll feel dizzy at the thought of the largesse that went into this house and garden.

Like all keen gardeners, he wanted instant effects, but, in his case, on the grandest of scales. While some of us buy large-ish (and therefore expensive) shrubs to fill corners, Holford bought in mature trees and had teams of workmen to plant them. In one staggeringly extravagant gesture he not only imported trees from China . . . he even brought a huge load of Chinese soil to ensure they would settle down happily in Gloucestershire!

He built the house and garden to entertain the royal, the rich and the celebrated of his day and he believed that the might of the Holfords would last for centuries. He was wrong. Today his great mansion is a girls' boarding school and the visitors are parents during term-time and, on rare open days, members of the public fascinated to see Victorian country house gardening at its grandest.

The elaborate Bath stone mansion dominates the scene, towering above marvellous garden architecture of beds and balustrades, terraces and staircases and the thrilling romanticism of the Italian garden with its lovely archway and intricate beds.

The terraces add to the atmosphere of formality and the trees heighten the mood, giant redwoods and tall cedars.

In the Holford days, the garden had a staff of 72 people. Today less than half a dozen full-timers and part-timers do the job. That means choosing labour-saving plants, utilising modern garden equipment whenever possible and sacrificing fussier effects.

I expect the detail of Mr Holford's garden in its heyday would have been dazzling, but the bones are fine and strong and handsome and make this an extra-special garden for those who admire high Victorian pomp at its most spectacular.

The school is just off the A438 Bristol/Bath to Tetbury road. Turn right from Bristol at the Hare and Hounds and the entrance is a few hundred yards along on the right. Westonbirt School gardens open on April 3rd and August 15th, 2–5 p.m. Admission 75p, children 25p.

GARDENS IN SOMERSET

Barrington Court, near Ilminster

Barrington Court in south Somerset marks an important chapter in the history of English heritage. It was the very first estate the National Trust received as a bequest.

And it has a place in the history of twentieth century English garden architecture because the great Gertrude Jekyll was called in to approve the layout in the planning stages.

Mind you, the National Trust found Barrington a mixed blessing when it received the place back in 1907. The trust had been gifted with a mansion and farmland in a sad state of disrepair . . . until 1919 and the arrival of the Lyle family of Tate and Lyle sugar fame who agreed to take over Barrington and restore it.

Colonel Arthur Lyle drew up a master plan for the restoration and improvement of Barrington. He restored the buildings, retaining the exterior of the sixteenth century manor but completely rebuilding the interior. He transformed the elegant seventeenth century stable block into a fine country house by commissioning a roof, chimneys and other details in the style of Edwin Lutyens, the architect who worked alongside Gertrude Jekyll.

This architectural hard graft needed one final flourish – a lovely garden. And Colonel Lyle pledged to make Barrington one of the finest in the West Country. He succeeded.

A master plan was prepared and, once it had been carefully examined and corrected by Miss Jekyll, the work began. You can see the plan at Barrington today . . . and you can step outside and see the plan in action.

This is a garden with big architectural bones around which a series of often stunning plant displays have been built and maintained. The bones are beautiful brick paths, shady pergolas, handsome walls and cool, elegant water features.

There are several clearly distinct areas which you are led through along formal paths and ways. Barrington offers a very, very big walled kitchen garden, the famous iris garden with its theme of blues and purples, the cool white garden with its tobacco plants, petunias, delphiniums and others taking up the theme, the hot-coloured lily garden with its very bright borders and, for me, the best of the lot, the magnificent South Lawn border, a mature border of beautiful plants with marvellous foliage to set off Barrington's best architecture.

There's a cool arboretum, a moat where the ducks swim and play and, above all, a marvellous sense of design and purpose in this showplace of formal between-the-wars English country house gardening at its best.

Barrington Court is in Barrington village, 5 miles north-east of Ilminster, off the A303, 6 miles south of Curry Rivel on the A378 between Taunton and Langport. The garden is open Saturday to Wednesday, April to October, 12–5.30 p.m. Admission £3, children £1.50. Plants for sale. Refreshments. The garden is suitable for wheelchairs.

Clapton Court, Clapton, near Crewkerne

Clapton Court is high on the Somerset garden visiting list. The ten acre garden and its adjoining nursery – and the licensed restaurant and tea room – attract more than 20,000 visitors a year.

Some are fuchsia lovers and others fans of pelargoniums, the pot geraniums. Clapton Court specialises in a wide range of both plants, with fuchsias ranging from the hardy, small-flowered varieties to the showy, large-flowered types and with a fine range of geraniums, some to be grown primarily for their flowers, others for the pungent scents of their leaves.

All this is to be found in the setting of a very well-run ten acre country garden which opened to the public in 1979 after some extensive restoration.

It took three years of back-breaking labour to show the delights of what had once been a splendid garden. Very good trees had become strangled by overgrown woodland, the stream which runs through the garden had become choked and beds and borders and other formal features badly needed attention.

In its very first year as a full-time garden to visit, Clapton Court won the Wilkinson Sword award for excellence and the garden has been improved even more in the years which have followed.

Clearing the woodland created glades where spring flowers now flourish in profusion, primulas and anemones in particular and where later flowering shrubs and bushes including azaleas and rhododendrons do very well indeed.

There is one truly venerable tree among the many rare and interesting specimens. It is the largest, oldest ash in England and it boasts the astonishing girth of 23 feet.

Clapton Court today is so well planted that it is impossible to visit the place at any time of year without finding some rare and interesting plant to enjoy, and that in a garden which prides itself on good labelling.

There are themed displays, among them the silver and grey plantings in the more formal areas around the house itself and a very good, new rose garden which often comes top of visitors' pops at Clapton. Roses or no roses, this is a garden which has interest throughout the year.

Clapton Court is 3 miles south of Crewkerne on the B3165 to Lyme Regis. Garden open March to October, Monday to Friday, 10.30 a.m. to 5 p.m., Sunday, 2–5 p.m., and Easter Saturday, April 2nd to 5 p.m. Admission £3, children under 14, £1. Refreshments, plants for sale at plant centre. Garden partly suitable for wheelchairs.

East Lambrook Manor, near Ilminster

Margery Fish's reputation as one of the great English twentieth century gardening writers and characters has gone into a slight decline these days . . . too homely, too Women's Institute, they say as the more literary stars like Vita Sackville-West rise to dizzier heights.

But Mrs Fish will be back, just as the bountiful, beautiful garden she built in a Somerset farmyard has come back from the threat of annihilation. Give it a decade or so and new generations will be enchanted by the writing and gardening of this remarkable woman.

Mrs Fish was once assistant to the all-powerful, tyrannical newspaper proprietor Lord Northcliffe before marrying one of his editors, Walter Fish of the *Daily Mail.*

With Hitler on the rampage and a fresh World War looking inevitable, the Fishes abandoned London in 1938, escaping the threats to the capital by buying a pretty Somerset manor. The journalist's wife knew precious little about gardening . . . but she liked the idea.

She liked the idea, in particular, of pretty, natural-looking, cottage-y gardens with nice beech hedges, cosy avenues, dense planting, attractive stone features.

And, by trial and error, she built the garden of her dreams, noting, photographing and learning all the time. Within a few years she had become a good gardener, within ten years she had made herself an outstanding gardener. She combined enthusiasm, knowledge of plants, flair and a bold sense of design and East Lambrook's garden grew and grew around her.

She quickly became a plantsman with a love for unusual and rare plants, trees and shrubs and she developed her style of profuse planting, of using self-seeding plants and of ensuring good flowers and foliage for all seasons in grounds cleverly arranged in a series of mini-gardens offering surprises and delights at every corner.

She talked and wrote about features in her creation, like the sparkling silver garden, so enthusiastically that she became a great hit on the garden club and WI circuits, influencing a whole new generation of women gardeners.

After her death in 1969, the garden very nearly disappeared. Planning permission for 23 bungalows on the site was granted. Thankfully a relative stepped in and the garden has now been restored and there is even a Margery Fish nursery attached where you can not only buy her delightful books but also descendants of the plants she introduced to the garden.

The garden is always a pleasure to visit and in high summer, with the full force of Mrs Fish's informal planting at its most colourful and opulent, East Lambrook Manor is an unforgettable sight, the picture of English cottage gardening at its most triumphant.

East Lambrook Manor is two miles north-east of South Petherton. Turn off the A303 to South Petherton, take the Martock Road and then turn left to East Lambrook at the bottom of the hill. East Lambrook Manor opens from March to the end of October daily, except Sundays. It is also open Bank Holiday weekends. Admission £1.90, OAPs £1.70, children 50p. Parties by appointment, telephone 0460-40328, fax 0460-42344.

Hadspen House, near Castle Cary

Hadspen House, like most good gardens with a bit of history, has had its ups and downs. Today it's on a high that has sent its fame across Europe and the United States.

This fine eight acre country house garden set against a wooded hillside in the rolling countryside of south-east Somerset was originally created in late Victorian and early Edwardian times and then restored in the 1970s by Penelope Hobhouse, one of our best-known gardening writers. She re-planted the old borders, sorted out the woodland with its mature, specimen trees, brought her own touches to the dramatic water garden and gave shape and form to the large walled garden.

After she left, Hadspen began to grow shaggy again . . . until a chance visit by a Canadian couple, Nori and Sandra Pope. Nori is a professional plantsman, Sandra a gardener with a rare eye for colour, texture and design and the two were touring England on vacation from their Vancouver garden and nursery business, visiting some of the famous and interesting gardens they'd read about. Hadspen was among them.

They walked the grounds and were deeply disappointed – and they didn't hesitate to tell the owner, pointing out where and why things were going wrong. Their visit couldn't have come at a better time . . . he needed a new gardener and promptly offered them the job. By the following day the Popes had decided that the adventure of re-creating a great English garden was too exciting to miss. They said yes.

That was back in 1986 and the Popes have a love/hate memory of their first months of cutting and clearing, hacking and burning the overgrowth. But slowly the details of Penelope Hobhouse's restoration and the original Edwardian garden emerged and blurred outlines began to focus into a fascinating whole.

But outstanding gardens must be more than re-creations. They're living, breathing places which need fresh ideas and that's what the Popes have done so brilliantly, blending a respect and delight in this garden's charming Edwardian bones with an extraordinary flair with plants and colour.

Just take a look at their now-famous walled garden border and you'll see why. Here Nori's plantsmanship and Sandra's eye for colour and texture blend together brilliantly in one of the triumphs of modern British country house gardening.

The border gently leads through a succession of colour changes from the palest pale to the richest, hottest colours in the gardener's palette and the planting is so clever that succeeding plants repeat the themes as the months go by.

The Popes have thrown snooty British prejudices to the wind. If their garden needs hot, showy, out-of-fashion dahlias, they'll use them and by doing so remind the rest of us that traditional dahlias like the coppery-leaved Bishop of Llandaff are beautiful plants in the right setting.

Nori even creates plants to help Sandra 'paint' her designs, developing new hybrids which have won Hadspen a reputation as an important independent nursery as well as one of the best gardens to visit.

Hadspen House is on the A371 Castle Cary–Wincanton road about three miles from Castle Cary. The garden opens 9 a.m. to 6 p.m., March to September 30th, Thursday to Sunday and Bank Holidays. Admission £2 adults, children 50p. Plants for sale. Teas Sundays and Bank Holidays. Partly suitable for wheelchairs.

Kingsdon, near Somerton

Patricia Marrow is the plantsman the plantsmen come to meet. They watch, listen, explore her Somerset garden and rarely leave her nursery of often rare and unusual plants without learning something new and bearing off some botanic treasure.

Nori Pope, who runs the nearby Hadspen garden with his wife Sandra, called one day and saw an extraordinary, lusciously decadent-looking crumpled purple oriental poppy growing at Kingsdon. Take it, it's just an accident, Patricia Marrow said carelessly. Nori Pope named it Patty's Plum in her honour and within a few years it has become one of Hadspen's better selling rarities.

Patricia Marrow's garden lies on the most difficult land imaginable for someone as keen on gardening as she is. Barely a spade's depth below lies solid rock. The only answer was to pack up and find a new home or to hack and delve her way through the unforgiving rock. She chose the tough option and called in heavy machinery to smash open troughs and holes which she filled with topsoil from wherever she could find it.

So this is a garden that dries all too easily when the sun shines and she is a perfectionist gardener who worries and becomes annoyed when her plants aren't looking their best. On one visit she taught me an invaluable lesson – that English gardens look and smell at their best when they're damp, even sodden. She learned the lesson the hard way in her difficult two acres.

It is a masterly garden, jam-packed with interesting plants arranged in charming, informal displays. She loves what she calls 'good plants', plants which work for their living by coming up each year with displays of good leaves and flowers.

She is very strong on foliage, loving ferns, hostas and the big spurges, for example, and there are lovely corners of green among the splashes of colour.

She raises hers from seeds and cuttings and is a self-confessed collecting maniac. She does English gardening a great service thanks to that passion, helping to preserve and pass on some of the loveliest garden plants which commercial nurseries can't or won't stock.

Patricia Marrow runs the garden as a business, but one she doesn't advertise. People come because they've heard of her by word of mouth or personal recommendation, and that's the way she likes it.

Kingsdon is two miles south-east of Somerton, off the B3151 Ilchester road. From the big Ilchester roundabout on the A303 follow the National Trust signs to Lytes Cary then turn left by Lytes Cary's gates and the garden is half a mile on the left hand side. Kingsdon is open by appointment, telephone 0935–840232. For charity openings admission is £1, children 25p otherwise entrance free.

Milton Lodge, Old Bristol Road, Wells

David Tudway Quilter declares that he has the best view of Wells and its cathedral. He's far too modest to say that he has the best garden in Wells, but both statements are true.

The setting of Milton Lodge is perfect, a rampart-like position buttressed by terraces on the Mendip edge with lovely Wells Cathedral nestling below and, a few miles across the Vale of Avalon, the striking sight of Glastonbury Tor and, beyond that, the rolling hills of south Somerset.

And the garden is as lovely as you'd like, a plantsman's paradise with good, hardy bones, beautiful trees and fine details set alongside a generously planted arboretum which will be one of the glories of Wells well into the next century and beyond.

Those bones – the grand yew hedges, the dramatic terraces and the magnificent viewpoints – date back to the early twentieth century when his grandfather Charles Tudway called in teams of workers to create the foundations for a new garden.

So when his grandson and family came to live in the house in the early 1960s, already a very keen gardener, he had a very good start to develop his interest in plants . . . but a lot of work to do.

By then the Milton Lodge garden, so admired between the wars that it was written up in *Country Life*, needed a great deal of attention. It had been taken over by a school for a while, and that almost always spells trouble for an established garden. It certainly did for these acres.

But neglected beds and borders give the keen gardener a chance to clear and raze and plant again and David Tudway Quilter seized the opportunity with relish.

Today Milton Lodge is that rare sight, a fully mature, large-scale private garden designed and planted with style and imagination and in full rein. Not every corner is just-so, but the care and good taste shown in both more formal displays like the handsome mixed borders and rose beds and the informal areas like the near-wild meadow where spring flowers abound make a beautiful display throughout the seasons.

From the moment you step out on the high terrace by the house with its row of Napoleonic War cannons – fired twice this century to celebrate the return of a son from the First World War and David Tudway Quilter's taking office as Mayor of Wells – you know you have arrived at a particularly beautiful garden. And you're right.

Milton Lodge is half a mile north of Wells city centre. From the A39 Wells–Bristol road turn north up the Old Bristol Road and the car park is on the left. The garden opens daily, except Saturdays, Easter to October 31st, 2–6 p.m. Admission £2, children under 14 free. Teas Sundays and Bank Holidays. Parties and coaches by written appointment.

Stapleton Manor, Martock, near Yeovil

Mr and Mrs Robert Sant are garden opening veterans, welcome examples of the generous folk who'll invite the public in to enjoy the fruits of their gardening labours and who get as much pleasure from their visitors as we do from enjoying displays as pretty and interesting as theirs.

Their manor home is an attractive Georgian hamstone house and when they came to live here back in 1960 the garden was attractive enough in a rather stiff, fussy, Edwardian way. But it wasn't their way.

Within nine years they felt happy enough with their re-working of these two-and-a-half acres to join the National Gardens Scheme and in 1990 they received their NGS award for 21 years of charity open days. They deserved every last plaudit.

By then they had simplified Stapleton Manor's stiff appearance and softened the look with design changes including widening the main lawn and grassing over unnecessary flower beds. Paths had been created, the garden worked into a series of compartments. Today it is in full maturity.

The Sants have much to show the visitors who enjoy the public openings at Stapleton Manor. Mrs Sant loves older roses, unusual plants and well-considered displays of shrubs and flowers while her husband enjoys creating colourful herbaceous borders and growing vegetables.

Which seems to me a useful combination of likes for two busy, interested gardeners. The result is a garden full of features – a bright-as-paint dahlia walk, many good rose displays, a grassy area nicely planted with small trees and shrubs, a pergola that boasts a wide range of climbers and a very good pool/bog garden.

There is close attention to the individual plants they have introduced to Stapleton Manor. Their grassed area boasts three different types of gum tree and flowering trees from as far afield as Argentina.

They collect plants on their travels and mementos from holidays or visits to friends include one or two flowers from the Canary Isles and lots of flowering plants from Corfu, all now thriving and flourishing in their new home in south Somerset.

Stapleton Manor is 1 mile north of the centre of Martock on the B3165 Long Sutton/Somerton road, 6 miles north-west of Yeovil. The garden is open Sundays July 4th and August 1st, 12–6 p.m. Plants for sale. Garden is suitable for wheelchairs.

Tintinhull House, Tintinhull, near Yeovil

The story behind the stately, much-loved garden of Tintinhull House in the picture postcard hamstone village of Tintinhull, near Yeovil is the story of three outstanding English women gardeners.

First was Gertrude Jekyll, the great Edwardian designer whose enthusiasm for the best plants and the most exciting colour schemes inspired the second, Phyllis Reiss, to create a garden along Jekyll lines in the two acres at her seventeenth century home in Somerset. The third, Penelope Hobhouse, today one of our foremost garden writers and designers, first saw Tintinhull in the early 1950s. That visit convinced her that she must become a serious gardener herself.

First Penelope Hobhouse restored the nearby Hadspen House garden at Castle Cary and then she and her late husband John Malins took over this National Trust garden, by then in severe need of attention.

She has worked a triumph. The setting of Tintinhull House is formal with that delightful house, good pavements, sound walls and mature hedges.

But the planting is gloriously informal. Penelope Hobhouse created her own rules as the garden developed under her tutelage and she has produced her effects brilliantly.

The garden is fairly traditional on colours. The centrepiece of the gardens-within-a-garden features two opposing borders, one hot with reds and yellows, the other a cooler display of blues, purples and pinks.

So far, so familiar. But look a little closer and you'll find wildly varying heights of plants which clamber and climb through each other alongside very astute use of unusual plants in unusual situations.

Just around the corner is the famous 'white' garden with its circular lily pond. Once it was dazzling white. Penelope Hobhouse has softened that brilliance with paler shades of planting.

She uses containers big and small. You'll find great pots of agapanthus to mark important viewpoints and clusters of more tender plants which can be whipped indoors when frosts threaten.

The delicacy of her rose displays is a delight. There's a particularly charming avenue of pale pink roses glimpsed from the central garden. Yet another example of what Penelope Hobhouse describes as 'informal gardening within a formal setting'.

At the time of writing Penelope has announced that she will be retiring from Tintinhull. Her heritage is two of the best gardens in Somerset and a worldwide audience for her books, her lectures and her thorough-going enthusiasm for the best in English gardening.

Tintinhull House is in Tintinhull, just off the A303 west of Ilchester. Follow the National Trust signs. The garden opens April to September, Wednesdays, Thursdays, Saturdays and Bank Holiday Mondays, 2–6 p.m. Admission £2.80. The garden is suitable for wheelchairs.

Wayford Manor, near Crewkerne

Wayford Manor and its three acre garden on a Somerset hillside is a place of beauty, charm and history.

The centrepiece is the house, a fine Elizabethan manor with a grand stone terrace which leads down steep stairs into the garden where you will find one of the best collections of decorative trees in Somerset.

This garden was re-designed by the great landscape gardener Harold Peto in 1902, one of a pair of historic gardens he made in this part of the world. The other was his own garden at Iford Manor, near Bradford-on-Avon, which you will find mentioned in the Wiltshire section of this book.

Iford has a classical theme to its terraces. At Wayford Manor, Harold Peto worked for a part-Italian, part-oriental feel and look.

The Italianate comes from the formal terraces and intricate stonework and statues which work so well in this setting. The oriental comes from the range of acers which were first planted when Peto was working here and which are being replaced as time goes by.

Wayford is also locally famous for its grand collection of magnolias and many brilliantly coloured rhododendrons and azaleas. If the weather is kind and the magnolias are spared burns from frost and cold winds, they make a marvellous sight, just as the flowering cherries make a spectacular show during their all too brief flowering period.

This is a garden of flowers and shrubs as well as trees, with a lot of emphasis on good bulbs to make springtime particularly magnificent.

There is a cool water garden, a moist bog garden, an area devoted to irises which was replanted in the latter 1980s and there are very attractive grass, stone and even wood-surfaced walks around the grounds to help you see the garden from all the best angles.

In 1990 Wayford was struck by 15 minutes of fury as those infamous gales tore into this ground, bringing down 15 mature trees. But this has meant a new chapter and a new beginning, because owners Robin and Wendy Goffe are replanting in the spirit of the original design thanks to research into Peto's original plans.

They are ensuring that one of the West's best private gardens will be thriving well into the next century.

*Wayford Manor is three miles south-west of Crewkerne off the
B3165 at Clapton or off the A30 Chard–Crewkerne road. The
garden is open 2–6 p.m., April 11th, May 2nd, 16th and 30th.
Admission £1.50, children 50p. Teas, plants for sale.*

Barrington Court Garden, Barrington, nr Ilminster.
A beautiful garden influenced by Gertrude Jekyll and laid out in a series of 'rooms'. Plants of interest through every season. Walled kitchen garden with vegetable and plant sales. Strode House Restaurant for a delicious range of hot and cold lunches using home grown vegetables from the kitchen garden. Afternoon teas.

Stourhead Garden and House, Stourton, nr Warminster. Britain's foremost landscaped garden with enchanting lakes and temples, rare trees and plants. Fine Palladian mansion, designed in 1721 for Henry Hoare by Colen Campbell. Many fine works of art. Spread Eagle Inn (N.T.), Village Hall Restaurant, N.T. shop and Reception Building at Stourhead Garden entrance.

Barrington Court Garden

The National Trust owns and cares for many more houses, gardens, historic sites, coast and countryside open to the public in the area. For details and opening times ask for the free Visitors' Guides to Avon and Wiltshire, Somerset or Dorset and South Wiltshire available from N.T. properties, N.T. shops, tourist information centres or write enclosing a s.a.e. to the Public Affairs Department, Dept GTV, Eastleigh Court, Bishopstrow, Warminster, Wilts BA12 9HW.

National Trust Restaurants and Tearooms. At many of the properties there are restaurants or tearooms which concentrate on home cooking and often serve local specialities. Some restaurants are licensed.

National Trust Shops in Bath, Bristol, Lacock, Salisbury and Wells. In addition many of the N.T. properties have shops. All offer a wide range of merchandise - much of which is exclusive to The National Trust.

Stourhead Garden

THE UK's MOST ACTIVE CONSERVATION CHARITY

GARDENS IN WILTSHIRE

The Courts, Holt, near Bradford-on-Avon

I don't know how I missed The Courts for so long. I'd been garden visiting in the Bristol region for at least ten years when two of my most admired gardeners were astonished to discover that I hadn't seen this Edwardian gem and warmly recommended it.

But part of the fun of The Courts is its sense of mystery and surprise once you've entered the place and the fact that it's a little out of the way and not one of the heavily tourist-ed National Trust gardens goes rather well with the garden itself.

The Courts is named after the village law court which used to meet in the house to decide cases involving local cloth weavers and their grievances. Today's garden was begun at the turn of the century with the planting of yew and box hedges and the mounting of stone ornaments.

Then, shortly after the First World War, the garden was developed by Lady Cecilie Goffe, a fan of the great designer Gertrude Jekyll and a complete believer in Jekyll's creed of creating a series of 'garden rooms'.

The National Trust were presented with the property during the Second World War and in the 1980s there was a marked improvement in this lovely seven acre garden thanks to hard work and increasing interest from garden writers and visitors alike.

There are a series of separate, delightful gardens-within-a-garden separated by yew hedges. The entrance is a deliciously shady avenue of pleached lime along flagstones which came from Devizes jail, the source of all the pavements at The Courts.

This leads to the Pillar Garden with its eight pillars which once held chains for drying cloth from the mill which used to stand by the house.

My favourite areas feature water . . . the Lily Pond garden with its canal-like stretch of water surrounded by grass walks and mature borders and, beyond that, the Lower Pond, into which the dye and waste from the old mill used to flow. This has become a shady, informal little corner with dappled light, good moisture loving plants and good trees.

There's a pretty Temple folly, some fine box sculptures, a semi-circle of yew as a focal point, a conservatory, a blue-

and-yellow border by the main lawn and a well-planted arboretum which sparkles with wild flowers among The Courts' many appealing features, but the main attraction is that surprise as you move from one area to the next to discover yet another delight.

The Courts is in Holt, 2 miles west of Bradford-on-Avon and south of the B3107 Bradford–Melksham road. The garden is open daily except Saturdays from April to October. Admission £2, children £1.

Easton Grey House, Easton Grey, near Malmesbury

Springtime is THE time to visit the garden at Easton Grey House in west Wiltshire.

The setting is pretty at any time of year . . . a delicate eighteenth century country house surrounded by a dreamy nine acre park and garden with views down to the young River Avon and the estate's own church complete with Norman tower.

There's a lot of history attached to Easton Grey too, for the house was a hunting lodge for the Prince of Wales in the 1920s and a decade before it was the scene of Prime Minister Asquith's fateful realisation that Britain must go to war with Germany as the First World War loomed.

Springtime sees brilliant riverside colours from the annually-cut willows as they send out their beautifully coloured new branches of gold and red.

But the real attraction of Easton Grey, and one that has had thousands flocking to the garden over the years, is the fabulous show of spring bulbs. It is Wiltshire's most famous daffodil garden and one glance during those brilliant weeks when they are at their best will show you why.

There are countless blooms . . . the garden has been planted with lorry loads, not wheelbarrow loads of daffodil bulbs and they make the most extraordinary sight.

Care is taken to ensure that the now established tradition of daffodil days never disappoint. Each year a sequence of colour photographs is taken of all the main daffodil areas and the pictures are closely examined to see if some patches are starting to look a little thin . . . the work of field mice if bulbs have been destroyed.

And if there are any signs of wear and tear, in goes another great load of bulbs to ensure that Easton Grey is top of the league when it comes to the vivid yellows of great daffodil displays. It makes an unforgettable sight.

The garden also offers good displays of lime-tolerant shrubs, many roses, lots of clematis and a large walled area with a traditional kitchen garden.

Easton Grey House is 3½ miles west of Malmesbury on the B4040 road. The garden is open all year except Sundays, Good Friday and over the Christmas/New Year period. Admission 50p, children are free. Teas. The garden is suitable for wheelchairs.

The Hall, Bradford-on-Avon

Dr Alex Moulton is renowned the world over as the outstanding inventor whose little-wheeled Moulton bike was one of the great British successes of the 1960s.

At a stroke he revolutionised the world of pedal power with his very different-looking two wheelers and everyone who was smart and trendy in the style-conscious Sixties was pictured on a Moulton bike, from Ministers to models and from pop stars to keep-fit keen company executives.

Home to Dr Moulton is a stunningly beautiful Jacobean mansion with fabulous stone terraces, tracery balustrades, topiary features and jewelled lawns, so quiet and peaceful that it is extraordinary to realise that the house is in a town and next door to his own bicycle-making works. It feels as if it lies deep in the countryside.

For that you have to thank the very inventive Dr Moulton. A little bit of thought, a clever piece of sleight of hand and some late twentieth century technology give The Hall its beautifully private, secluded feel.

Just peer into the shadows behind the trees which face the noble facade of The Hall and you'll find one very non-Jacobean feature . . . Dr Moulton's remarkable 'baffle' wall. It is an extraordinary idea and it works perfectly.

The tall, high tech wooden baffle not only hides the workplaces that lie just the other side of the garden boundary, it also mutes the sounds so efficiently that you're barely aware this garden's real position in a busy part of town.

And it has stood the test of some pretty damaging winds. The baffle needed no more than running repairs after the great gales of 1990.

The baffle helps visitors to concentrate on this garden's glorious charms. It is an architectural garden, a place for peace, quiet and contentment. Chairs and benches are set at strategic points so visitors can stop and admire the elegance surrounding them.

There are very good trees, particularly the handsome row of Irish yews, and one of summer's big attraction is the large, rustic pergola smothered with very free-flowering rambling roses.

The Hall is near the town centre, on the B3107 and opens only occasionally. For opening details, see NGS and local press.

Hazelbury Manor, Box, near Bath

Hazelbury Manor's Grade II listed garden is a brilliant affair, a triumph of the boom years of the 1980s when its then owner, the flamboyant developer Ian Pollard whose successes included the gleaming *Observer* newspaper building just south of Chelsea Bridge in London, chose to lavish his riches on the grounds surrounding his Elizabethan home.

Like some moghul emperor he decreed a grandiose garden with the richest of lawns, great rockeries, a magnificent topiary garden depicting a full chess set, a formal Elizabethan rose garden, a foliage garden, a species rose walk with more than 100 different roses and a sequence of colour-themed borders.

He called for a mini-Avebury of megaliths carefully aligned in a stone circle to echo the prehistoric ruins not far away on the Wiltshire Downs.

He ordered his staff to restore the manor garden's pre-war features, the laburnum-covered avenue and the spring garden with its hazel walk and beech walk.

And he set them work tidying up such historic features as the genuine medieval archery walk complete with its teller's seat for the chap keeping the scores as the arrows flew home.

The 1980s are over and the staff who delved, dug, designed and planted are gone along with their master in this colder financial climate, but this extraordinary monument to Eighties' extravagance should last a while yet.

Hazelbury Manor impresses from the moment you approach the place. There is a wonderful drive down a hillside and the manor comes into view seen through great gates. It is a beautiful and historic house – Elizabeth I knighted five gentlemen in the Great Hall when her Royal Progress halted at Hazelbury – and it was lovingly restored earlier this century.

That was when the outline of the garden you see today was laid with its wide, impressive main lawn edged by deep borders and tall hedges and the smaller compartment gardens beyond.

The 1980s revolution brought a softer approach alongside those more formal features with a love of small-scale decoration and pleasing plants, particularly around the house itself.

Hazelbury fascinates me as a garden. At a time when everyone was striving for labour-saving effects it dazzled as a labour-intensive masterpiece. When gardens were being run on a shoe-string and a man-and-a-half, Hazelbury boasted four full-time gardeners and an armoury of the latest and best equipment and know-how.

I hope its effects can linger . . . it is a spectacular and rare example of intensive late twentieth century English country house gardening and no visitor leaves without being astonished at its luxury.

Hazelbury Manor is five miles west of Chippenham. From the A4 at Box, take the A365 Melksham road and, at the top of the hill, turn left on to the B3109 and left again after a few hundred yards. The garden opens daily May to September and at weekends in April and October. Teas available. Admission £2.80, OAPs £2, children £1. National Garden Scheme weekends are May 1st and 2nd and July 24th and 25th. Plants for sale on charity days. The garden is suitable for wheelchairs. Coaches welcome. Telephone 0225–812113.

Iford Manor, Iford, near Bradford-on-Avon

Head gardener Leon Butler has a burning ambition – to make Iford Manor nothing less than the best garden in Wiltshire. Well, it's certainly one of the best . . . and one of the best architectural gardens in England, for that matter.

This ravishing garden set in a deeply wooded Wiltshire valley with the trout-filled River Frome sparkling just below the main entrance is the work of the great Edwardian designer Harold Peto. One of his partners was the young Edwin Lutyens, one of the major influences on early twentieth century English garden design.

Peto believed that the best gardens should be a beautifully worked combination of good architecture and good plants, and that's what he set about to create at Iford Manor when he bought the manor house in 1899. He declared: 'Old buildings or fragments of masonry carry one's mind back to the past in a way that a garden of flowers only cannot do'.

He certainly had some marvellous old masonry to install in his new home . . . a genuine Roman sarcophagus, ancient classical columns collected on visits to the Mediterranean, some eighteenth century German hounds, a statue of a boy by Grinling Gibbons, examples of thirteenth century Italian sculpture and a great deal more besides.

Between 1899 and 1914, when the garden was completed, he worked these marvellous pieces of masonry into a series of terraces, cleverly using both open prospects with full sunshine and shadier areas with dappled light to create his hauntingly romantic garden.

The mood is deliciously Italian – there are corners which come straight from the garden of some sun-drenched palazzo – and the fact that this little bit of the Mediterranean is to be found lodging in a leafy English valley makes it all the more exciting.

Leon Butler has been head gardener at Iford since the late 1960s and he has dedicated much of his working life to restoring Iford to pristine condition for its owners Mr and Mrs J. Hignett. He only uses the sort of plants available to Peto and he has helped add new touches like the shady, peaceful Japanese garden with its large rocks and whispering waterfall.

Lutyens who, with his partner Gertrude Jekyll, has become one of the towering giants of twentieth century European gardening was very much a junior to Peto. But it is 'Ned' Lutyens' name which most inspires garden-lovers. That's all wrong, Leon Butler says firmly and he is doing all he can to prove by the example of Iford Manor that Peto was the master and Lutyens the student.

Iford Manor is a couple of miles south-west of Bradford-on-Avon. It is signposted on the A36 Bath–Salisbury road between Freshford and Beckington. Or from Bradford, drive through Westwood and then to Iford. The garden is open May to September, Tuesday to Thursday, Saturday and Sunday, Summer Bank Holidays and Sundays in April and October, 2–5 p.m. Admission £2, OAPs, students and children under 10, £1.50.

Lackham Gardens, Lacock, near Chippenham

Lackham college of agriculture by the postcard pretty village of Lacock is an education for any gardener, from the out and out novice to the expert, plantsman or garden historian.

The large gardens are not only a delight to visit for their year-round interest, they also serve as an educational exercise for both the students at the agriculture college and the thousands of visitors who take advantage of the college's open door policy.

There is so much to see and do at Lackham that it's advisable to give yourself a little longer than you would at most gardens to visit, and if you're looking for a place to take a party of garden enthusiasts, this should be very high on your list of attractions to see.

My favourite features are the long, deep, profuse mixed borders which demonstrate perfectly how to vary size and colours and forms in a mixed display. Catch them at the right time of year and you will be delighted by the sheer generosity and the skill of the planting.

Other big effects include the pleasure gardens which offer a very good collection of roses and which shows, simply and effectively, how today's roses have developed.

The greenhouses are packed with interesting plants like a giant fruited Citron tree and other exotics and you will find interesting experiments too, like the area in the walled garden devoted to showing the biological control of garden pests under glass.

Visitors who like unusual plants will be struck by many to be found at Lackham including the brilliantly variegated form of summer jasmine which casts a golden glow in one corner of this fascinating garden.

Romantics will be very pleased with the Willow Pattern pool and bridge echoing the famous china design and woodland lovers will enjoy the pretty woodland walks which have been created to lead visitors to the riverside as well as the large bird viewing hide.

Springtime sees beautiful displays – I have a lasting memory of long grass on the approach to the garden nodding with countless snakes head fritillaries – and that level of interest continues throughout the seasons at a garden that shouldn't be missed.

And, to round it off, there is a coffee shop, an adventure playground and many, many plants for sale.

Lackham Gardens is three miles south of Chippenham. The garden is well sign-posted from the main road. The garden is open daily Easter to November, 11 a.m. to 4 p.m. Entrance £3.15, concessions £2, children £1, family ticket (2 adults, four children) £8.40. Plants for sale and refreshments. The garden is suitable for wheelchairs.

Sheldon Manor, near Chippenham

Sheldon Manor was already beautiful long, long before gifted rosarian Major Martin Gibbs began adorning these grounds with his collection of old roses.

The house dates back to the thirteenth century and the outbuildings and architectural features have grown around it over the centuries, always dominated by a group of ancient yew trees which still overlook the formal gardens at the front of the house.

There is a well-worn flagstone terrace, grand old walls, fine lawns and handsome hedges and the scene is so dramatic that it's no surprise to learn that Sheldon is regularly used for open air plays. It suits the more romantic Shakespeare comedies perfectly.

But for keen garden visitors Sheldon Manor means one particular plant . . . the rose. Major Gibbs was one of the early champions of the revival of interest in old-fashioned roses, loving their subtler, more delicate flowers, their varied foliage forms and their habit of flowering for a short period

86

each year rather than repetitively, allowing the emphasis to shift to other plants as their season arrives.

His superb collection dates back more than two decades and, now in its maturity, it shows the great range of effects that can be achieved by old roses in a variety of settings, from formal to the near-wild.

The most breathtaking display comes in June and July when the large number of ramblers and climbers he planted years ago in the old orchard start working overtime. Some are now flowering 20 and more feet above the ground and everywhere you'll find flashes of red, white and pink high above you.

He doesn't rest on the laurels of his now long-established collection. New additions are made all the time and there are always signs of new plantings.

The Manor and the garden are run as a family enterprise with both Major and Mrs Gibbs cooking home-made buffet lunches for visiting parties. The magnificent house is open to the public.

And for garden lovers there is much to see besides that rose filled orchard. The garden offers a pleasing blend of formal and informal areas with impressive features like the pleached hornbeam hedge.

The garden architecture and ornaments are very special with warm Cotswold stone walls and a collection of very large copper pots which were once milk vats used for making cheese which came from Holland a century ago.

Don't miss one very rare old rose. It grows on a wall in front of the house. It is a pink rambler and none of England's top rosarians have been able to identify this survivor from Edwardian days, so it is now known as the Sheldon Rose. If ever a garden deserved a rose of its own, this one does.

Sheldon Manor is 1½ miles west of Chippenham off the A420 Bristol–Chippenham road. The manor is clearly signposted from the main road. The garden is open Sundays, Thursdays and Bank Holidays, from April to October 10th, 12.30–6 p.m. Admission £1.75, OAPs £1.50. Refreshments, plants for sale. The garden is suitable for wheelchairs.

Stourhead Garden, Stourton, Wiltshire

When the starry-eyed banker Henry Hoare returned from a heady grand tour of Europe and decided to create a corner of classical paradise on the Wiltshire/Dorset border, he did the world an enormous favour.

Hoare had fallen in love with the paintings of Claude and Poussin with their sensual landscapes of classical ruins in lovely valleys peopled by scantily-clad beauties and he wanted a dream world of his own. And that is what he created.

I first saw Stourhead as a teenaged schoolboy on a sketching party and my love affair with the place has never faltered. I've seen it in hailstorms, snow, breathless drought and the sparkling colours of spring and it always enchants.

This eighteenth century masterpiece with its lovely follies of temples and grottos, cottages and leafy lanes, glorious trees and beautifully-tended lawns and, as the centrepiece, a sparkling lake which reflects one of the finest tree plantations you'll see in such a compact area, is a delight from start to finish.

It is best to walk the garden the way Henry Hoare led his guests when this estate was being built in the 1740s. He would walk from the house, not from where the busiest entrance is these days, by the Bristol Cross.

The walk from the house leads by stately lawns to a woodland path that gives increasingly dramatic views across and down to the pleasure garden.

The garden was designed to be seen at first from a distance, a lovely set-piece which so enchanted visitors that they couldn't resist making the effort to walk down to such delights as the grotto with its statues of Neptune and a water nymph.

In summer the air is heavily scented by the yellow azaleas and the view is a riot of colour from the Victorian plantings of rhododendrons. Purists sniff at all this colour in an eighteenth century garden and it's true that efforts have been made to pull that blazing display further and further back from the lake where its effect was doubled by the water's reflections.

But I like the rhododendrons just as I like the glorious collection of flowering shrubs and beautiful trees that help to make Stourhead such a dreamy place to visit. After five minutes in Henry Hoare's masterpiece, it's perfectly possible to forget that the late twentieth century exists.

Best of all, round off your visit with a quick drink in the Spread Eagle pub just opposite the lower entrance by the Bristol Cross and, if you look at the window closely enough, you'll see the names of David and Primula Niven etched on the window. The film star and his wife stayed here during the Second World War and loved Stourhead so much that they couldn't resist leaving their signatures, carved with a diamond ring.

Stourhead has had that sort of effect on its lovers for two-and-a-half centuries.

Stourhead Garden is 2 miles north-west of Mere on the B3092 Mere–Frome road. The garden is open throughout the year 8 a.m. to 7 p.m. or dusk if earlier. Admission March to October £4, children £2, parties £3.40 per person; admission November to February £3, children £1.50. Refreshments, shop. The garden is suitable for wheelchairs.

Stourton House, Stourton, near Mere, Wiltshire

It takes a lot of nerve to open a flower garden bang opposite the entrance to one of the most famous landscaped gardens in Western Europe . . . but the Bullivants have never been short of enterprise and courage.

The millions of visitors who've travelled to Stourhead over the past couple of decades cannot have failed to notice a big, brave show of blue and pink hydrangeas on a grassy bank just before they arrive at the Stourhead car park. That is the shop window of the Bullivants' empire.

Their garden is just off the very large National Trust car park for the Stourhead visitors. Some people visit Stourton House in mistake for its noble neighbour – and have a thoroughly nice time too. Best of all is to allow yourself a little more time than usual and take in both Stourhead and its friendly neighbour.

Anthony and Elizabeth Bullivant's delightful four acre, informal flower garden with its soaring views over the chalk countryside to Mere Down is the perfect contrast to Henry Hoare's landscaped masterpiece just across the lane.

The Bullivants are honest-to-goodness English country gardeners, but with a flair that has made them famous. Elizabeth Bullivant has a dried flower business with outlets in America and Kuwait while Anthony Bullivant, a retired Army officer, has a passion for interesting plants and bulbs – he'll wax lyrical over his collection of speciality daffodils and hydrangeas . . . the couple have more than 200 varieties of hydrangea.

The garden is divided into a series of loosely defined areas with a dramatically different centrepiece. This is the eye-catching formal garden surrounded by magnificently tall, sculptured hedges. Surely a marvellous inheritance from previous owners? Not on your life! Look closer and you'll discover that the hedges are the result of their clever cutting of the fast-growing, much-derided Leylandii.

Stourton House garden offers very good ideas in almost every corner, from that Leylandii topiary to the tasteful use of both usual and unusual plants in every corner of this garden.

And then there are the Bullivants themselves, always enthusiastic, always as eager to hear advice as to give it and, best of all, always ready to lead visitors to the best shows of plants and flowers that day. If you're really lucky, their very free-ranging hens will have laid that day and there will be eggs, as well as plants, for sale.

Stourton House is 3 miles north-west of Mere just off the B3092 Mere–Frome road. It is open from 11 a.m. to 6 p.m. every Sunday, Wednesday, Thursday and Bank Holiday from April to the end of November. Admission £2, children 50p. Coffees, teas, plants for sale. The garden is suitable for wheelchairs.

Pound Hill House, West Kington, near Chippenham

The very best place to experiment with plants is not in greenhouses or carefully controlled beds . . . it's out in the rough and tumble of a real garden. Practical trial and error will help you find the places where each plant looks and grows most happily.

That's the philosophy Barbara Stockitt has pursued since she and her husband Philip decided to start their own nursery business behind the pretty garden at their home in the little village of West Kington, between Tormarton and Chippenham.

She has always been a keen gardener – her brother is the rose grower David Austin, famous for his range of finely-scented 'modern' old-fashioned roses which have the helpful habit of repeat-flowering, unlike the true old roses with their once-a-year-displays. Barbara Stockitt has set aside one area as a pale rose garden with clipped box edging, and many of the beauties you'll find growing so happily there are Austin creations.

91

The two acre garden, which she began creating in the 1970s has been divided into areas with clear themes. The vegetable garden has pretty, interesting-looking vegetables so that it manages to be both productive and attractive at the same time.

The open garden with its sweep of lawn has generous borders where herbaceous plants are tried and tested in the open to see how they grow and how well they look alongside other plants.

Barbara Stockitt is a great enthusiast for container gardening and the paved areas around her fifteenth century Cotswold stone home have a fine collection of well planted pots and containers of every size using a very wide range of plants including agapanthus, arum lilies and unusual pelargoniums.

This garden never stands still. As her nursery business expands – she supplies plants to top centres as far afield as London and northern England – so the garden changes as new plants are introduced. She has now opened a little plant centre at West Kington for retail customers and she enjoys showing visitors how their plants will look by taking them to the bed, border or container where they are growing happily in her own garden.

Typically, on my last visit she was planning to completely re-shape one major border area and to build herself an ambitious water garden. On my next visit I know she'll have some fresh scheme in mind. That's Pound Hill . . . a truly dynamic English country garden.

Pound Hill House and plant centre are in West Kington, 8 miles north north-west of Chippenham and 2 miles north-east of Marshfield. In the village take the No Through Road at the crossroads. The garden is open March 1st to December 1st, Wednesday to Sunday and all Bank Holiday Mondays, 2–5 p.m. Admission £1.50, OAPs £1. NGS openings April 11th and July 18th. The garden also opens jointly with Manor Farm May 30th and September 5th, £2 combined admission, £1.50 OAPs. Plants for sale and the garden is suitable for wheelchairs.

THE GARDENS
AT A
GLANCE

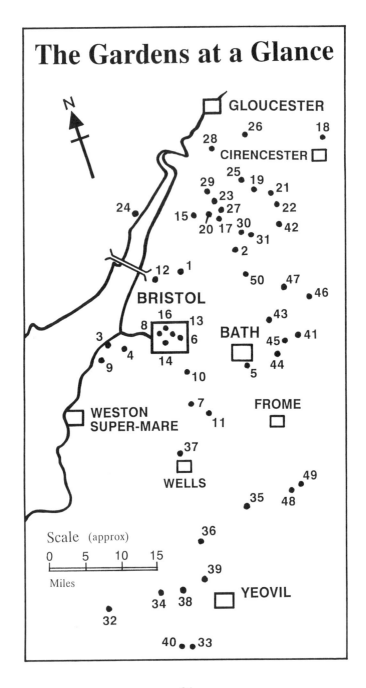

The Gardens at a Glance

N

GLOUCESTER

• 26   • 18
• 28
CIRENCESTER □

• 25
• 29   • 19   • 21
• 23   • 22
• 24   • 27
• 15   • 30   • 42
• 20 • 17   • 31
                 • 2

• 12 • 1
• 50   • 47
BRISTOL   • 46

• 16   • 13
• 8   BATH   • 43
• 3   • 14 • 6   • 45 • 41
• 4   □
• 9   • 44
• 10   • 5

• 7   FROME
WESTON   • 11   □
SUPER-MARE □

• 37
□   • 49
WELLS   • 48
              • 35

• 36

Scale (approx)   • 39

0   5   10   15   YEOVIL
                            □
Miles
                     • 34 • 38
• 32

• 40 • 33

94

Key to the Gardens

(Please see the garden entries for directions)

AVON

1 Algars Manor
2 Badminton
3 Brackenwood
4 Church Farm
5 Crowe Hall
6 Goldney Hall
7 Harptree Court
8 Hillside
9 The Manor House,
   Walton-in-Gordano
10 Parsonage Farm
11 Pear Tree House,
   Sherborne Garden
12 Portland Lodge
13 9, Sion Hill
14 Bristol University
   Botanic Garden
15 Urn Cottage
16 Vine House

29 Stancombe Park
30 Westonbirt Arboretum
31 Westonbirt School

SOMERSET

32 Barrington Court
33 Clapton Court
34 East Lambrook
   Manor
35 Hadspen House
36 Kingsdon
37 Milton Lodge
38 Stapleton Manor
39 Tintinhull House
40 Wayford Manor

GLOUCESTERSHIRE

17 Alderley Grange
18 Barnsley House
19 Beverston Castle
20 Brackenbury
21 Chipping Croft
22 Hodges Barn
23 Hunts Court
24 Lydney Park
25 Minchinhampton
   Gardens
26 Misarden Park
27 Newark Park
28 Painswick Rococo
   Garden

WILTSHIRE

41 The Courts
42 Easton Grey House
43 The Hall, Bradford
   -on-Avon
44 Hazelbury Manor
45 Iford Manor
46 Lackham College
47 Sheldon Manor
48 Stourhead
49 Stourton House
50 Pound Hill House